Regent's Study Gu
General Editor: Paul S

Under the Rule of Christ

Dimensions of Baptist Spirituality

Published by Regent's Park College, Oxford OX1 2LB, UK
in association with Smyth & Helwys Publishing, 6316 Peake Road,
Macon, GA 31210, USA

Printed in the United States of America.

The paper used in this publication meets the minimum
requirements of American National Standard for Information
Sciences—Permanence of Paper for Printed Library Materials.
ANSI Z39.48–1984 (alk. paper)

Under the rule of Christ : dimensions of Baptist spirituality

Library of Congress Cataloging-in-Publication Data

general editor, Paul S. Fiddes.
p. cm. -- (Regent's study guides ; 14)
Includes bibliographical references and index.
ISBN 1-57312-498-2 (pbk. : alk. paper)
ISBN UK 978-09539746-4-1
1. Spirituality--Baptists.
I. Fiddes, Paul S.

BV4501.3.U525 2007
248.4'861--dc22

2007025433

Cover illustration: *Peace Be Still* by He Qi (1998).
Reproduced by kind permission of He Qi, www.heqigallery.com

Preface illustration: *White Crucifixion* by Marc Chagall (1938).
Reproduced by kind permission of Art Institute of Chicago;

Regent's Study Guides

Under the Rule of Christ

Dimensions of Baptist Spirituality

Paul S. Fiddes
(Editor)

Regent's Park College, Oxford
with
Smyth & Helwys Publishing, Inc.
Macon, Georgia

Dedication

To the members of the
Baptist Union Retreat Group
who have fostered contemplation
and who asked for this book

Contents

White Crucifixion by Marc Chagall (1938)

Preface

This book had its beginnings in a letter addressed to the Principals (or, for American eyes, 'Presidents') of the six colleges in membership with the Baptist Union of Great Britain. It came, in 2004, from the Baptist Union Retreat Group (BURG), and asked whether the Principals could devote themselves to writing on the theme of spirituality among Baptists. They were glad to take up the challenge, and their gratitude for the invitation is shown in the dedication of this book. It is thoroughly fitting here to acknowledge the contribution of BURG over many years to the fostering of contemplative prayer among Baptists.

During the past fifteen years or so the Principals have committed themselves to various joint writing projects, as an expression of the companionship they enjoy together and as a public sign of the partnership between the colleges.[1] The colleges in London, Oxford, Bristol, Manchester, Cardiff and Glasgow value an increasing closeness of working together in formation of men and women for ministry and in serving the churches. They have a common concern for the central place of spiritual growth in the development of ministers, and have been glad of the opportunity of this particular writing project to reflect on the theme together. It should be stressed that this is not, therefore, a collection of disparate essays. The book is the result of five meetings, some overnight and all including prayer together, in which each chapter was planned, read and revised corporately. It is hoped that the reader will pick up many connections between the chapters, some explicit and some silent, which bear witness to the sharing in mind and heart that lies behind the finished book. In addition, the Principals tried out their chapters at the 2006 Consultation of 'Baptists Doing Theology in Context' held at Luther King House, Manchester, and comments from participants there have also shaped the whole.

There have, of course, been changes in the group of Principals from time to time over the past fifteen years, and this project has proved to be no exception. Christopher Ellis left the Principalship of Bristol Baptist College to accept a call to a local church pastorate as the project was in mid-stream. The group is delighted that he has nevertheless offered a completed contribution to the book, and at the last hour his successor at

Bristol, Stephen Finamore, has shared in the first chapter. Aptly, his piece draws upon his experience as a minister in a local Baptist congregation.

The preface illustration shows the painting 'White Crucifixion' by Marc Chagall. It depicts a world 'under the rule' of Christ, in two senses. The cross carries the inscription in both Latin and Hebrew, 'Jesus Christ, King of the Jews', indicating rule as power and authority; but the crucified figure also acts as a rule in the sense of a 'ruler' to measure things, laid flat over the landscape of turbulent events beneath it. This is Christ, the measure of all things, Christ as the rule of a life which—as the picture makes clear—is often marked by suffering.

This book proposes that the spirituality of Baptists, in all its diversity, is characterized by living 'under the rule of Christ'. All Christian spiritual traditions, of course, affirm this truth, but this book suggests that there is a particular sense of being under Christ's rule which has been shaped by the story of Baptists and by their way of being church through the centuries. Spirituality has been moulded by an ecclesiology where the local congregation stands under the direct rule of Christ without intermediate authorities. Such an understanding of church has had an impact on all the dimensions of spirituality which are shared with other Christian traditions, and even on those which have been fostered within more monastic 'rules' of life. It has shaped the particular kind of attention to the 'other' and to the triune God as the infinitely 'Other' which this book also proposes is characteristic of spirituality.

It would be a misuse of Chagall's painting, however, not to be aware of the circumstances in which it was created. It was Chagall's reaction, as a Jew, to the terrible events of the *Kristallnacht* of 9 December 1938—the 'night of broken glass'—when many thousands of Jewish homes, shops and synagogues were destroyed in Nazi Germany. The painting depicts also the stories of other attacks on Jews in the past, including those in Chagall's home town of Vitebsk on the borders of the Russian empire. The painting shows houses overturned, synagogues desecrated, scrolls of the law burnt, refugees fleeing, and Jews forced to wear shameful signs of identity.

Much of this anti-semitism was fuelled by the Christian church, and so there is a deep irony in using a symbol—the crucified Christ—taken from the persecutors to express the suffering of the artist's people.[2] But

Christ, we notice, wears the *tallith* or Jewish prayer shawl as a loincloth. Chagall thus presents the crucifixion as a universal symbol of suffering, whether Jewish, Christian or of any other kind. It would be invidious to compare the much smaller story of Baptists under persecution with that of the Jewish people, for there can be no comparisons in suffering, but there is nevertheless a fellowship in suffering through the ages. This book suggests that the Baptist sense of being under the rule of Christ has been strongly marked by the experience of oppression, especially in the early days of Baptist life.

Finally, however, Chagall presents the rule of the crucified Christ as a symbol of hope as 'a shaft of light enters the painting and we are led to believe that there is a path of hope to be discovered among the wreckage of this world's events'.[3] There is a stillness about the figure of Christ which compells attention, amid the turmoil of events and the journeys of life which surround him. Spirituality 'under the rule of Christ' must be connected, this book affirms, with the mission of God in the world to bring about peace and justice for all. These chapters will have succeeded in their aim if readers rediscover, through them, that Christ is truly the rule or measure of all things.

Notes

[1] Previous joint publications have been Paul S. Fiddes (ed.), *Reflections on the Water. Understanding God and the World through the Baptism of Believers*. Regent's Study Guides 4 (Macon: Smyth & Helwys Publishing / Oxford: Regent's Park College, 1996); Richard Kidd (ed.), *Something to Declare. A Study of the Declaration of Principle of the Baptist Union of Great Britain* (Oxford: Whitley Publications, 1996); Richard Kidd (ed.), *On the Way of Trust* (Oxford: Whitley Publications, 1997); Paul S. Fiddes (ed.), *The Baptist Way of Doing Theology* (Oxford: Whitley Publications, 2001).

[2] This irony has been well explored in the study of Chagall by Graham Sparkes which is included in Richard Kidd and Graham Sparkes, *God and the Art of Seeing. Visual Resources for a Journey of Faith*. Regent's Study Guides 11 (Macon: Smyth & Helwys Publishing/ Oxford: Regent's Park College, 2003).

[3] Graham Sparkes, 'Marc Chagall: Playing with Fire' in Kidd and Sparkes, *God and the Art of Seeing*, p. 49.

Contributors

Revd Dr **Christopher Ellis** was Principal of Bristol Baptist College until 2006, and is now minister of West Bridgford Baptist Church, Nottingham. He is a specialist in the study of Baptist Worship, and his recent book *Gathering. A Theology and Spirituality of Worship in Free Church Tradition* (2004) is widely used. He is also the author of *Together on the Way. A Theology of Ecumenism* (1990). At present he teaches a course on the interaction of theology and spirituality at the University of Nottingham.

Revd Professor **Paul S. Fiddes** is Principal of Regent's Park College in the University of Oxford and Professor of Systematic Theology in the University. His books include studies on the doctrine of God (*The Creative Suffering of God*, 1989; *Participating in God*, 2000), the atonement (*Past Event and Present Salvation*, 1989) and the interface between theology and literature (*Freedom and Limit*, 1991; *The Promised End*, 2000). He has also recently published a book on Baptist principles, *Tracks and Traces: Baptist Identity in Church and Theology* (2003).

Revd Dr **Stephen Finamore** is Principal of the Bristol Baptist College. In the past he has been a labourer, a lawyer, director of a community development project in inner London, a rural development worker in the Peruvian Andes and pastor of a local church. His doctoral work was on the Book of Revelation, and he was one of the contributors to a recent book on Baptist contributions to the theme of following Jesus in a violent world (*Expecting Justice, But Seeing Bloodshed*, 2004).

Revd Dr **James Gordon** is Principal of the Scottish Baptist College, in Paisley, before which he held full-time pastorates in Glasgow, Paisley and Aberdeen. Previous publications include *Evangelical Spirituality: From the Wesleys to John Stott* (1991) and an intellectual biography of the Scottish theologian James Denney. Current research focuses on the Scottish spiritual tradition and journal writing as a form of theological and pastoral reflection.

Revd Dr **Richard Kidd** is Principal of Northern Baptist College, Manchester. He has been a Baptist minister for more than thirty years, and for the last twelve years Principal of the College. He co-authored an earlier Regent's Study Guide, *God and the Art of Seeing*, and theological reflection on art remains his main area of research and writing. He is now working on a further volume in this series which will focus specifically on the relationship between art and prayer.

Revd Dr **John Weaver** is Principal of the South Wales Baptist College. Previously he was Director of Pastoral Training at Regent's Park College, Oxford, and before that pastor of Highfield Baptist Church, Northamptonshire. His previous publications include two volumes in the *Regent's Study Guide* series (*In the Beginning God—Modern Science and the Christian Doctrine of Creation*, 1994; and *Outside-in: Theological Reflections on Life*, 2006) and *Earthshaping Earthkeeping: a Doctrine of Creation* (1999). Once a university lecturer in Geology, he has a continuing interest in the theology of creation and the environment.

Revd Dr **Nigel Wright** is Principal of Spurgeon's College in London, and was formerly minister of Altrincham Baptist Church. Among his publications are studies of Baptist life and thought (*Challenge to Change*, 1991; *New Baptists, New Agenda*, 2002), books on Christian doctrine (*The Radical Kingdom*, 1986; *A Theology of the Dark Side*, 2002) and studies on the relationship between the church and the state, in which he has a particular interest and expertise (*Disavowing Constantine*, 2000; *Free Church, Free State: the Positive Baptist Vision*, 2005).

1
Baptists and Spirituality: a Rule of Life

Paul Fiddes and Stephen Finamore

1. The concept of spirituality

Paul S. Fiddes

'Spirituality' is a notoriously slippery concept. Sometimes today it is used merely as a non-specific term for 'religion', and many people seem to find it a more acceptable word to own for themselves than either 'religion' or the naming of a specific faith such as Christianity or Islam. It seems an especially convenient term in an age in which many people construct their own religion from different elements, drawn from east and west, rather than being committed to a particular historical tradition of faith. In a survey conducted by the Alister Hardy Institute, 63% of respondents in the UK claimed to have had an experience 'with a spiritual content' at some time in their lives,[1] and other commentators have estimated that as many as 90% regard themselves as 'spiritual beings'.[2] The benediction from the Star Wars films, 'May the force be with you!', is a fitting mantra for this pervasive and vague sense of spirituality. It appears that a wide range of people can agree that 'spirituality' is a vital part of life, even when they are not sure how it relates to religious faith. The National Health Service in the UK, for instance, is happy to train nurses in being sensitive to a general 'spirituality'.

Is 'spirituality' then simply a more respectable word for religion, or might it be a distinct dimension within the complex of practices, beliefs and experiences of religious individuals and groups? If it *is* a distinct element, then how is it to be identified? In the past, 'spirituality' did bear a limited meaning. In the seventeenth century, for instance, the term tended to be used as equivalent to 'asceticism', so contrasting the life of the spirit with the life of the body and even denying the body. This meaning was rooted in the long ascetic tradition within Christianity, which found special expression in the life of the monastery. In the earliest monastic movement, individual hermits, seeking solitude, attempted to rival each other in the excesses of their self-denial, so that spirituality became something of a competition. The predominant image was one of warfare against the forces of evil, in which the battleground was conceived as entirely internal, characterized as the lusts of the flesh and the devil. Extreme mortification of the body was the chief spiritual weapon, and the abiding symbol of this movement in the popular imagination has been Simon Stylites, sitting on top of his pillar for 47 years. In contrast to this early monasticism of a solitary existence, St. Benedict had a powerful impact on the formation of monastic community, in which the ascetic impetus was controlled by being held in a common life, with a common rule.

Asceticism is not, however, the obvious sense in which 'spirituality' has been widely employed in the past century. Rather than reinforcing a dualism of body and spirit, it has been seen as affirming the wholeness of embodied existence, and several of the contributions in this book take wholeness and integration as being the key mark of spirituality. John Weaver takes a definition from William Stringfellow, that 'Biblical spirituality encompasses the whole person in the totality of existence in the world, not some fragment or scrap or incident of a person.'[3] Chris Ellis takes a similar approach in his chapter, citing Philip Sheldrake to the effect that 'Spirituality is concerned with the *conjunction* of theology, prayer and practical Christianity.'[4] Nevertheless, the aspect of a disciplined life-style that characterized the ascetic movement does often still accompany an appeal to spirituality. In line with this, the earliest use of the term in fifth century Christianity (*spiritualitas*) had an ethical connotation, describing the transformed quality of the life of Christian believers who had received the gifts and graces of the Holy Spirit. In this sense it related to *sophia*, or communion with divine wisdom which shapes a life of virtue.

Another positive aspect to be retrieved from the ascetic sense of spirituality is a resistance to the reduction of the meaning of existence to the world of the senses. The term 'spirituality' is readily understood today as expressing the 'reaching out' of the whole person towards realities which transcend the physical senses, without depreciating the material body. This usage has the advantage of being applicable to various religions, and indeed to non-religious experience as well; it might denote *any* awareness of 'mystery at the heart of life' that cannot be contained within empirical-scientific explanations of the world. However, when placed in the context of religious attitudes, beliefs and practices, this meaning is difficult to distinguish from religion generally.

Practices of prayer are often closely connected with 'spirituality', and in some uses of the term ('spirituality and worship') it seems that they are practically synonymous. In particular, spirituality is associated with more contemplative practices of prayer, centring upon stillness of heart, meditation, and a movement towards a sense of the presence of God that leaves words behind. These practices are often given the label 'mystical' and connected with medieval spiritual writers such as Julian of Norwich, Richard Rolle and St John of the Cross. While it is unlikely that such writers would have identified a particular experiential state called 'mysticism',[5] they were certainly aiming to get beyond both the 'positive way' of images and the 'negative way' of reversing human experience, in order to reach an encounter with the God who is final mystery. This mystery was to be found at the point where deep awareness of the self and awareness of God coincided, so that it was not possible—in Julian's words—to 'tell the difference'. She knew very well, of course, that there *was* an infinite difference between the Creator and the creature; the point was that there was no language in which the difference could be 'told'. Something of this tradition is continued in a modern spiritual writer, Kenneth Leech, who writes of spirituality as a knowledge of our self which prepares us for the adventure of knowing God at work in the world.[6]

A key meaning of 'spirituality' is thus a heightened sense of the presence of God which is inseparable from the mission of God. In this book, my own chapter concentrates on spirituality as giving attention to the presence of God and others, and reflects on the characteristic aspects of 'journey' and 'stillness' to which this attentiveness leads in Baptist life. Richard Kidd continues the theme in his chapter by focusing on the place that attention to suffering plays within Baptist experience in the past and the present, in England and in the world church. He suggests that there is something typically Baptist about beginning from the attention to the suffering of fellow-disciples and moving from there to engagement in the sufferings of Christ. In his chapter John Weaver shows that there is a deep link between attention to the body of Christ in the Eucharist and in a Baptist church meeting, and argues that both are the foundation for mission as the broken body in the world. Further, the final chapter by Chris Ellis insists that spirituality for Baptists is bound up with commitment to God's mission, and that attention to the love and grace of God are the strongest motivations for mission rather than fear of numerical decline of the church.

Most of the dimensions I have identified above—discipline, wholeness, prayer, moral transformation, transcendence of the senses, and a heightened sense of attentiveness to God and others—are contained in the idea of a 'rule of life', taking classic form in the Catholic church in the rules for monasteries and other religious orders. These rules aimed to define living in community, to moderate the denial of the body, and to place worship at the heart of life through the disciplined use of the daily office. They have had an effect on Christian living which has crossed the boundary of the walls of the monastery or religious house, and over the years modified versions have been adopted by those who are neither priests or monks, either as individual Christians or in 'Christian communities in the world' holding to a common rule of life. It is worth reflecting a little, then, on what this tradition can offer to us in our quest for the distinctive nature of spirituality. In case Baptist readers become anxious about giving such attention to Catholic orders, they should be assured that after the next section the whole book is indeed about 'dimensions of *Baptist* spirituality'. But the point of telling this story is to see what Baptist spirituality has inherited from the larger story of the church, and how the appeal to the 'rule of Christ' by Baptists has its own particular character.

2. The rule of Christ and rules of Religious Orders

One of the earliest set of rules for monastic life was written by St Augustine in the fifth century, in a letter (no. 211) addressed to a community of women where his sister had recently been Prioress, and in two sermons (nos. 355 and 356) delivered to dispel suspicions aroused by the fact that the clergy of Hippo were leading a monastic life with him in his bishop's residence. The sisters are to 'dwell in the house with oneness of spirit', and 'let [their] hearts and minds be one in God'.[7] Along with domestic instructions Augustine commends a life of poverty and mutual forgiveness, with moderate discipline, and strikes the note that is characteristic of all subsequent rules: prayer in common occupies the central place, comprising hymns, psalms and readings at stated hours of the day. Those sisters who want to lead a more contemplative life are allowed to use the oratory to follow special devotions in private, but corporate prayer is at the heart of an ordered life.

The nuns are to be obedient to the Prioress, but Augustine urges 'let her cautiously impose rules' and 'let her be more anxious to be loved than to be feared by you'.[8] Faults in the sisters are to be discerned by the sisters themselves, 'by the witness of two or three.'[9] They are bidden 'call not anything the property of any one, but let all things be common property'.[10] Similarly, the clergy living with Augustine as monks are to hold all things in common and to own nothing individually (citing Acts 4:32ff).[11] Augustine expects them to keep the rule of the house by their own motivation, as a matter of mutual trust in a context of relative freedom, and he is disappointed when they let him down.[12] We notice that while the nuns and monks of Roman Africa looked to Augustine as their spiritual father Augustine belonged to no order and founded none, exerting no authority as the 'Superior' of a monastic family. His 'rule', expanded by later material from other sources,[13] nevertheless exercised a strong influence on other rules, including that of St Benedict and the Augustinian orders of the Middle Ages named after him.

In the rules that followed, the note of obedience is sounded much more strongly, along with adherence to poverty, chastity and mutual charity. Theologically, this is obedience to the rule of Christ, but it takes form in strict obedience to the Superior of the monastery who represents Christ, while in the rules of the Middle Ages obedience is also to be offered to the church and the hierarchy of bishops. The predominant image in the Rule of St Benedict (c. 530AD), which sets the tone for all later rules, is that of the Abbot as a father to whom obedience is owed, for 'he is the representative of Christ in the monastery, and for that reason is called by a name of his.'[14] Here the name 'father' is unexpectedly applied to Christ himself.[15] The hortatory prologue speaks of the rule of Christ, announcing that 'we are about to found a school for the Lord's service' and addressing itself to those who 'giving up your own will, take up the strong and most glorious weapons of obedience, to fight for Christ, the true King'.[16] Stress is laid on the formation of character through obedience; by persevering in the monastery until death, disciples will be conformed to the new man in Christ, and will become 'partakers of Christ's kingdom'. But obedience takes concrete form in submission to the Abbot, who is the father of the monastic family.

Benedict's aim, it must be said, is to moderate the excesses and rivalries of bodily self-denial to which solitary monks had subjected themselves; a more balanced and stable spiritual life is achieved by the control of austerity by the Superior, and by sinking the individual in the life of the community. The Superior is commanded to teach nothing except the 'precept of the Lord' and to take counsel with the brethren before making a decision. Nevertheless, the word of the Superior is to be obeyed without delay 'as if it were a divine command'.[17] Common prayer, in the divine office, is held seven times daily ("as the prophet says, 'seven times in the day I will praise thee'"),[18] and 'nothing is to be preferred to it'. This is the 'work of God' (*opus dei*), but other labour is also encouraged—bringing farming, building, biblical scholarship and school teaching within the scope of the spiritual life in this extended family within the monastery walls.

While the central image of Benedict's rule is of obedience to a father, in the medieval rule of St Francis the image is obedience to the pattern of Christ's life as revealed in the Gospels. The earliest form of Francis' rule (written in 1209) seems to have been little more than a collection of texts from the Gospels, probably including Matthew 19:21, Matthew 26:24 and Luke 9:3.[19] Francis did not take as his model any monastic order, but simply the life of Christ and his Apostles, stressing abandonment of wealth, following the example of Christ and an apostolic ministry of preaching: 'The rule and life of the Friars Minor is this: to know how to follow the Holy Gospel of our Lord Jesus Christ, living in obedience, without possessions, and in chastity' (Rule of 1223).[20] As a symbol of this obedience in poverty, chapter two of the rule allows for the wearing of shoes only when 'compelled by necessity'. The great impulse given to foreign missions in the thirteenth century is due to St Francis, who was himself a missionary in the East. In this he revived, though probably unknown to him, the early monastic life of the Celtic church which followed the rules of St Columbanus and St Columba, and was marked by a strongly missionary zeal exercised by travelling monks. Francis' rule is a pattern for a mendicant life rather than the settled contemplative community of St Benedict.[21] By using the Roman breviary for the divine office the clerical brothers would share in the common prayer of the church wherever they might be on their mission.[22]

It seems that Francis intended that if any brother sinned in a less than mortal way, and owned it humbly, the priest should be permitted to apply no greater penance than the command 'go and sin no more',[23] although this merciful treatment is generalized in the rule as actually written (chapter vii). Nevertheless, obedience to Christ is mediated through obedience to the Superior and to the church. The third rule of 1223, written under the direction of Francis when the order had greatly increased in numbers, begins with the declaration that: 'Brother Francis promises obedience and reverence to our Lord Pope Honorius and his successors canonically elected and to the Roman Church. Let the other brothers be bound to obey Brother Francis and his successors.'[24] The rule concludes by firmly binding together obedience to the church and conformity to the pattern of Christ the poor man: 'Being always obedient and submissive at the feet of this same holy church, we may observe the poverty, the humility and the holy Gospel of our Lord Jesus Christ.'[25]

The rule which St Ignatius of Loyola created for the Jesuit Order is attached to the *Spiritual Exercises* (c. 1541) which have exerted an extraordinary influence on the formation of people's spiritual life, far beyond the borders of the order and among evangelicals as well as Catholics.[26] To the ordered round of the daily office prayer,[27] Loyola adds the practice of a periodic retreat organized over four 'weeks',[28] when the individual works with a spiritual director who is expected to adapt the Exercises to personal needs of the person undertaking them. The image in the book is of the Christian knight or soldier, who is obedient to Christ as his King and Leader. The aim of the Exercises is 'to conquer oneself and regulate one's life', offering a method by which to overcome one's unruly passions and, by gaining control over every conscious act, acquiring inward peace. The soul's election *of* Christ coincides with its election *by* Christ, and the making of the resolution to follow Christ on the way of self-conquest at the end of week two (illumination) is strengthened by the exercises of the third week, in which the Gospels are read in a meditative way.

In recent years these exercises in a spiritual reading of scripture (the *lectio divina*) have been perhaps the most influential part of Ignatius' work, encouraging the reader to place him or herself in an imaginative way within the Gospel scenes where we see Christ walking before us to his cross. This obedience to Christ, held in the visionary imagination, is nevertheless placed in the context of obedience to the church, Ignatius declaring in his rule that 'all judgement laid aside, we ought to have our mind ready and prompt to obey, in all, the true spouse of Christ our Lord, which is our Holy Mother the church hierarchical'.[29] Ignatius grounds this obedience in a doctrine of the Holy Spirit, believing that 'between Christ our Lord, the Bridegroom, and the Church, His Bride, there is the same Spirit which governs and directs us for the salvation of our souls.'[30]

3. Baptists and the rule of Christ

The rules of the monasteries and other orders, centred upon Christological images of the father, the man of poverty and the leader of soldiers, highlight the response of obedience to Christ, together with a detachment from worldly wealth and an ordering of the day by a pattern of common worship. Though they all mention mutual subjection of the brothers or sisters to each other, they clearly channel the rule of Christ through the rule of the Superior and the hierarchy of the church. Here, while we may learn much from the spirituality of the monastic movement, we may contrast a distinctly Baptist version of the rule of Christ. John Smyth in his *Principles and Inferences* (1607) begins by explicitly replacing 'religious societies . . . [such] as Abbeys, monasteries, nunneries . . .' with 'the visible church', declaring that 'a visible communion of saints is of two, three or more Saints joined together by covenant with God and themselves'.[31] The local congregation stands directly under the rule of Christ, and this means that his rule is also committed to the whole community.

The liberty of local churches to make decisions about their own life and ministry is thus not based in a human view of autonomy or independence, or in selfish individualism, but in a sense of being under the direct rule of Christ who relativizes other rules. As John Smyth puts it, a true church bears the marks both of 'communion in all the holy things of God' and 'the power of our Lord Jesus Christ'.[32] With regard to this power, 'the church which is Christ's body hath power from Christ, and the Eldership . . . hath power from the body.'[33] This liberating rule of Christ is the foundation of what makes for the distinctive 'feel' of Baptist congregational life, which allows for spiritual oversight (*episkope*) both by the *whole* congregation gathered together in church meeting, and by the minister(s) called to lead the congregation.[34] Oversight flows to and fro between the individual and the community, and there is no legalistic definition of the balance between them, everything depending on mutual trust.

The freedom of a local church from external ecclesiastical government because it is under the rule of Christ differs from John Locke's notion that a church as a voluntary society has the freedom to make its own rules and prescribe its own membership qualifications.[35] As the Declaration of Principle of the Baptist Union of Great Britain (1904) puts it, every local church 'has liberty to interpret and administer [Christ's] Laws'. Moreover, since the same rule of Christ can be experienced in assemblies of churches together, there is also the basis here for Baptist associational life, and indeed for participating in ecumenical clusters. The London Confession of 1644 depicts the associating together of churches in the body of Christ, and it follows the Separatist *A True Confession* of 1596 in applying to congregations the covenant language of 'walking together' under 'one and the same Rule'. Just as oversight flows in a two-way manner between individual and community, so it flows between the individual church and the community of churches. Because it stands under the rule of Christ, the local congregation can never have decisions imposed upon it from outside; but because the churches together stand under the same rule, the single congregation must always listen carefully to the other churches in its task of finding the mind of Christ:

> And although the particular Congregations be distinct and severall Bodies, every one a compact and knit Citie in it selfe; yet are they all to walk by one and the same Rule, and by all meanes convenient to have the counsell and help of one another in all needfull affaires of the Church, as members of one body in the common faith under Christ their onely head.[36]

The Separatist and later, Baptist, conviction was that through covenant a local community stands under the immediate rule of Christ and so has been given the power to elect its own ministry, to celebrate the sacraments of baptism and the Lord's Supper (the 'seals of the covenant'), and to administer spiritual discipline or the authority to 'bind and loose' (Matt. 18:17). This threefold authority is often related to the threefold ministry of Christ as prophet, priest and king.[37] In the monastic code obedience is offered to the Superior and ultimately 'the hierarchical Catholic Church' as having the power to bind and loose: that is, to assure people of the forgiveness of sins or—when wilfully unpenitent—to exclude them from the Lord's Table.[38] Here among early Baptists this power is given 'to the body of the church, even to two or three faithful people joined together in covenant'.[39]

This version of the rule of Christ has significance not only for church order but for the spiritual life. The issue of assurance of salvation haunted the Puritan mind, prone to despair in the face of a sovereign God; how could a believer be sure that he or she was indeed one of the elect and part of God's covenant? Calvin himself had simply appealed to the existence of faith as assurance enough, but English Puritan theology followed the trend that sought to find more visible evidence of election, that is in the living of a life that was obedient to the commandments of God recorded in the scriptures.[40] This stress on personal obedience, often called 'experimental Calvinism', converged with an interpretation of the second commandment that identified idolatry with any humanly devised worship and ministry, and with a portrayal of Christ as the new Moses, giving rules for the government of his church. As the earliest systematic theologian of Puritanism, Dudley Fenner, expressed it, faithful obedience to the commandments of Christ about the ordering of his church brings God's people 'into a covenant of life and blessedness'.[41] Spiritual discipline of members and true church order were thus regarded as marks of salvation, assuring the believer of membership within the covenant.

In a later chapter in this book, Nigel Wright explores in more detail the ecclesiology of early Baptists and the place of church discipline within it. Existing under the rule of Christ, he suggests, means that expectations of membership today should be upgraded into embracing a corporate rule of life. Following him, James Gordon in his chapter works out the way that the whole community of believers stands under the rule of Christ as revealed in the scriptures, so that reading the Bible is never individualistic. Standing under the rule of the Word as both Christ and scripture leads, he argues, to the characteristic Baptist tension between individual liberty and the discipline of the community. We may judge that, like the monastic rules, development in the spiritual life has been seen among Baptists as a community matter. Our concern for church order may not arise from the same anxieties about predestination as our ancestors, but we can learn from them and from the monastic tradition that spirituality, in worship of God and obedience to Christ, is not a matter of merely individual experience but a churchly matter. In his chapter, Nigel Wright suggests that the stress on the 'community of disciples' in the Anabaptist tradition was in fact a kind of 'laicized monasticism'. This sense of community, together with the Anabaptist stress on 'following Jesus' (also something learned from the monastic experience) has, he argues, had a profound effect upon Baptist spirituality.

This was an insight recovered by Dietrich Bonhoeffer, in his creation of a community of pastoral formation during the Nazi period in Germany. In urging the making of 'a new type of monasticism which only has in common with the old an uncompromising allegiance to the Sermon on the Mount' he writes:

> A Christian needs another Christian who speaks God's Word to him. He needs him again and again when he becomes uncertain and discouraged, for by himself he cannot help himself without belying the truth. He needs his brother man (sic) as a bearer and proclaimer of the divine word of salvation. He needs his brother solely because of Jesus Christ. The Christ in his own heart is weaker than the Christ in the word of his brother.[42]

Bonhoeffer also makes clear that Christian community is not the wish-fulfilment dream of any individual who envisions a community according to his or her own ideals. The sooner we are disillusioned by the 'unhappy and ugly' aspects of any actual community the better, for 'by sheer grace God will not permit us to live even for a brief period in a dream world'.

Living in illusions makes us into accusers of others when they seem to fall short of our imagined aims. Christian community is not a human ideal that we must realize, but is a gift of God: 'it is a reality created by God in Christ in which we may participate'.[43] Bonhoeffer sees this truth applying to a local church as much as to a theological college, and thereby recaptures something of the reality of the church as pre-existing individual faith, as assumed by the monastic rules.

Conversely we can see the local 'visible communion of saints' taking visible form in new kinds of community life under the rule of Christ. One example is the Northumbria Community in the UK, in which Baptists have both participation and leadership.[44] Setting itself in the tradition of Celtic monasticism this community embraces both the contemplative and apostolic (i.e. missionary) aspects of the Celtic movement. The community consists of some companions living in the mother house and many more dispersed into the world, but all banded together by their common vows and common vision. The Community Rule is 'to say Yes to availability and vulnerability as a way of living'. This involves availability to God in contemplation and to each other in hospitality, while intentional vulnerability is expressed by being 'teachable in the discipline of prayer, saturation in the scriptures and being accountable to one another, often through soul friendships'.[45] At the heart of the community, whether gathered or dispersed, is the Daily Office of Morning, Midday and Evening prayer, a 'regular cycle of daily prayers which constitutes the essential rhythm of life around which other activities can take their proper place'.[46] Like the breviary among the Franciscans, the common office can be used wherever a companion of the Community might be.

This modern example draws on several traditions of community life—Celtic, Roman, Eastern[47] and Jewish[48]—for the making of a new form of community. It is also possible to offer a local congregation a similar breadth of spiritual experience, opening its eyes to the riches of the Christian heritage. What concludes this introductory chapter is the case of a Baptist church in Bristol, described by its former pastor, with some reflection on the way that Baptists reacted to being exposed to the wider spirituality of the catholic or universal church. The reader is invited to envisage the events recounted, in the light of some of the principles introduced earlier—such as the corporate and regular offering of prayer, obedience to the rule of Christ, the liberty of the church in ordering its life and worship, commitment of members of a community to each other, and the use of the imagination.

4. A practical experiment in spirituality
Stephen Finamore

When I was first called to be the minister at Westbury in north-west Bristol, my initial discussions with the church's deacons suggested that one of their key priorities was the deepening of the spirituality of the congregation. There was a sense of dissatisfaction with models of prayer which had been inherited and a desire to explore some alternatives. Together we took a number of different initiatives.

Firstly, we organized a series of home group studies based on Richard Foster's book *Celebration of Discipline*.[49] Later on I led a series of morning services based on Robert Warren's *An Affair of the Heart*.[50] During these series we introduced the congregation to a number of prayer exercises. There were several other activities including fresh approaches to reading the Scriptures, Saturday prayer breakfasts, and midweek prayer meetings with different styles. However, the single biggest change we made was the use of the evening service.

The pattern I inherited after a relatively long pastoral vacancy was one in which the evening service was a smaller version of the morning one but without any attempt to cater for the presence of children. We decided there was little point in doing the same thing twice, to accept that the evening service was going to attract smaller numbers, and to use the time to experiment with different Christian traditions of worship in order to learn from the approaches to spirituality which they represented. Things we found helpful might be occasionally incorporated into the morning service where others could enjoy them.

The morning service became a more eclectic affair which drew on the most popular songs, prayers and activities of different traditions, predominantly our own, while the evening services tended to take one specific approach and to see it through consistently. Over the years we added different kinds of services to our repertoire and found that they each offered different windows onto God and onto God's world. In each case my goal was to find a team of people within the church who would take responsibility for planning and leading acts of worship in the style they particularly enjoyed. This was more successful in some cases than in others. Most were held on a termly basis, that is three times a year.

In addition, our involvement in our local *Churches Together* group gave us an opportunity on a quarterly basis to share evening worship with one of our ecumenical partners in a united service. We were fortunate to be in partnership with nine other churches and were able to learn from their traditions. These ranged from the local Community Church to the Catholic Parish church. The meeting circulated round the churches and in each case its organization was a matter for the host congregation.

In our termly cycle, we first held a series of 'praise' services, modelled on the styles of worship associated with the 'Spring Harvest' festival, influenced by the charismatic renewal movement. We would be led by singers and musicians at the front of the church using lots of newer songs interspersed with brief prayers and acclamations. Many songs learned for this service subsequently found their way into the repertoire of songs we used on Sunday mornings. By contrast, another termly series offered songs and prayers in the Celtic tradition. For these services we used liturgies and songs from the Iona and Northumbria communities, ecumenical communities which draw on the Celtic tradition of spirituality from a Reformed and Evangelical perspective. The sermons would often be based on stories of the Celtic saints. Again, the songs, along with some of the prayers were successfully introduced to the larger morning congregation. A sequence of services offering evening prayer from the Protestant and Catholic Taizé community, with repetition of short pieces, some in English and some in Latin, was rather different from the style to which the congregation was used, but was deeply appreciated. The choir enjoyed learning the new material and many warmed to a quieter, more reflective approach to singing.

Youth services were always the responsibility of the Young People's Fellowship and their leaders. The style of the service varied considerably over the years depending on the interests of the teenagers within the church at the time. In the weeks ahead of the service we would divide the young people into groups with different responsibilities: music, drama, artwork, prayer, co-ordination and so on. The first few youth services were dominated by the band who played lots of newer songs very loudly. One service featured a smoke machine which was used far too enthusiastically. There was always lots of drama, use of video, DVD and computer graphics and so on. More recently the youth services became less frantic affairs, often taking the form of a 'café church', the congregation seated around tables in comfortable chairs with quieter worship and a more reflective style. At the beginning of these services the participants were offered tea, coffee or a soft drink along with doughnuts and biscuits. They spent the first few minutes simply chatting to other people on their table. Then someone was introduced who sang a song and someone else told a story. People were invited to talk at their tables about the issues raised by the story. There were more songs and poems, refills of coffee and more opportunities to talk together, and the service ended with prayer.

We tried to run a Children's 'Fun Day Service' three times a year as a way of reaching out to local children. The Fun Days ran on Saturdays with the children and their parents then being invited to tea and a 45 minute service on the Sunday. One of these was held near 5th November (Guy Fawkes Day) and would be followed by fireworks. The songs would be the simple ones the children had learned the day before with lots of actions and movement. Prayers and talks were kept short, simple and to the point.

'Alternative worship' went under the title of 'Explore'. The team responsible for preparing these services worked tremendously hard to find fresh and innovative ways for us to find the presence of God among us. In one instance, a tent was pitched in the church. After some meditative material members of the congregation were given the opportunity to visit different installations, one of which was the tent. There is something incongruous about entering a well-known space and finding it wholly re-organized, with a large tent pitched in the middle. People become curious and are drawn to investigate. Sometimes they will find the courage to pray in new ways because the new space seems to open them to new possibilities. Such a new space for worship was also provided by the installation of a huge block of ice as the centre-piece of another service. We sat on chairs and on floor cushions gathered around it. In the semi-darkness it reflected light in unusual and unexpected ways and in gradually melting it helped us to reflect on the transitory nature of so much in our experience. In other services the central space was surrounded by projected images, to aid reflection on the particular topic chosen for the service, such as journey, stillness, and resurrection. Labyrinths were marked out on the floor to enable the participants to walk on a way of pilgrimage and to pause for meditation at places marked by a symbol for remembrance. At other times meals were held in groups round small, low tables during the service.

All these were ways to try to break down our expectations and to give us new space in which we might be encountered by God. The services are quite difficult to describe, as their impact exceeded the power of words. I recall one such happening being repeated as a workshop at an event involving churches from the regional association. Those who had participated reported to me that, on the basis of what they had read about the service beforehand, they had expected to be nonplussed or even antagonistic, but that having shared in it they found the whole experience extremely helpful.

Our church used the denominational hymn book, *Baptist Praise and Worship* (1991) as its principal source of hymns, supplemented by increasingly more songs, mostly newer ones, from other sources. Plenty of members of the congregation retained affection for the older version of the *Baptist Hymn Book* too (1962, affectionately known as 'The Green Book'). They liked the old and familiar words and they appreciated some of the fine hymns which failed to make it into the more recent collection. One series of evening services thus took the form of what some disparagingly call a 'hymn-prayer sandwich'. A more positive approach would see it as a dialogue between God's word and people's response, with an overall sense of movement and purpose.

Then there were services in the style of the popular television programme *Songs of Praise*, in which participants speak about their lives and the significance of certain hymns for them. I have attended many churches which include a time in the service for people to 'testify', to come forward and talk about something that is happening in their relationship with God. Attempts to introduce this at Westbury brought mostly silent embarrassment. However, ask a group of people each to choose a song which they have found helpful, and to introduce it by saying what it means to them, and you suddenly have people sharing moving experiences of the way God has been working—or not working!—in their lives.

Some evenings were set aside for 'services of healing'. There was some doubt in my mind that anyone would come forward for prayer at Westbury. It was not our way. I looked for a way to make it possible. This might not be appropriate at churches where the culture is to seek prayer at the end of most services, but it worked for us. We would share a quiet communion service and rather than distribute the elements as is our normal practice, people were asked to come forward in groups to receive them. As the deacons served the congregation, two men would stand two or three yards to one side of the table and two women the same distance from the other. People were told that after they had received communion they could either return to their seat or walk to either side of the table. They did not need to say anything, and in this case general prayers would be said, or they could speak quietly to those ready to pray with them. In neither case would the content of the prayers be heard by the congregation. People were welcome to come forward to seek prayer for themselves or for someone else. While those who wished were being prayed for, the singers and musicians performed quietly and the rest of the congregation could either listen, sing or pray silently with those who had stayed at the front for prayer. This quiet and gentle approach seemed to break down barriers and make it possible for people to feel safe enough to seek prayer without feeling they were drawing undue attention to themselves.

Other services took the form of guided prayer. A small team would prepare material and lead a service of quiet reflection and meditation. When nothing else was scheduled I tended to organize a service that I called 'evening prayer' and which was relatively easy to organize. The main feature of this was an extended period of shared intercessory prayer towards the end of the service. We would try to find creative ways to encourage people to participate, sometimes by the lighting of candles, sometimes by inviting the mentioning of subjects for prayer followed by silence and then a sung response such as one of the brief Iona or Taizé songs. More and more people found it possible to join in.

An annual event was 'prayer round the building'. On the first Sunday of the year it became our practice to pray for the use of our building. We would start with songs and prayers in the sanctuary and after a reading we would set off singing for the church hall. When we had gathered again we would be led in a prayer for all the activities that were scheduled to take place there over the coming year. We would then move through all the larger rooms in the same way. Then we would divide into groups to visit the smaller rooms before reuniting to go back together into the sanctuary for communion. The service gave a strong sense of linking our Sunday worship with the service and mission activities of the church.

Another yearly event was lessons and carols by candlelight, an opportunity to fill the building with several hundred night-lights and hear appropriate Scripture readings and sing traditional carols. This was not very different from what goes on in many churches, except that we set outdoor candles on the path up to the church and placed big outdoor candles with large flames on the flat roof over the main entrance so that there was a real sense of event, and so that the theme of light breaking into the darkness was presented before people came into the building. After the service fruit punch and mince pies were served to people as they left the church so that people stayed and gathered in groups and talked to one another. Perhaps this was a picture of God's hospitality and his work of building friendships.

One of my fears about this process was that we might become rootless and unsure of our identity as Baptists. Another fear was that the services might become exhibition pieces rather than acts of worship. I do not think either of these things happened. What tended to happen was that as we became accustomed to a particular tradition we would shape the way we used it so that it became an expression of our identity before God. Rather than lose our identity we found a deeper sense of who we are in God.

In addition, I was concerned that the use of varied styles of evening service might result in our regular attenders lacking the sense of continuity, and the sense of being engaged in a shared journey, which rightly belongs to being regularly a part of a congregation. This was addressed in two associated ways: through the liturgical year and through the lectionary. While our congregation had no wish to be constrained by the church year which is often seen by Baptists as an alien imposition on their practice, we agreed there was benefit in marking it in some ways. We celebrated the major festivals of Christmas, Easter, Pentecost and Harvest with all-age services, often with shared meals afterwards. These services included lively songs, dramatic sketches, lots of congregational participation and some interactive worship material. Likewise we found ways to mark the Sundays of Advent and Lent. In addition we registered the changes in the liturgical year by changing the banners at the front of the church. There is one used in Advent, one for the Christmas season, one for Lent, others for Easter, Pentecost and Harvest. These were all designed by members of the congregation, and can be viewed on the church website.[51] The purpose was not necessarily to insist that every service take its theme from its place in the liturgical year but to provide a backdrop to the worship life of the church which would ensure that we were constantly reminded both of the flow of the year and the great events of the Christian story.

Continuity was also provided by the lectionary. Where appropriate, the evening services, whatever their character, were built around themes which emerged from the lectionary readings set for the date. We would nearly always include the set Gospel reading and the Psalm even if neither of these was preached on. Apart from the intrinsic value of these readings, the Gospel in particular provided a means of linking services to one another which were otherwise quite different in tone and style. The lectionary readings were never just *imposed*, however, on visiting speakers or on church members who were responsible for particular services. Furthermore, I always made it clear that I reserved the right to abandon the lectionary readings if I felt there was good reason to do so, and I occasionally did. There were some questions about the lectionary in church meetings where all these issues were discussed. The case for the readings was made in terms of our need for continuity and in the fact that they encourage ministers to preach on the whole of the gospel story and on different parts of the Scripture, and not to keep returning to particular favourite texts.

In fact I need not have worried so much about continuity, which was mainly provided by the people who attended. While different services did attract different groups within the church as a whole, there was always a core of people committed to the process of deepening our relationship with God by using different liturgical traditions as windows onto God.

When I first became involved in Baptist churches in Battersea in inner London as the seventies became the eighties, I was struck by a degree of insecurity in our practice. We did not do what we did out of any particular conviction that it was right but because it was a way of distinguishing ourselves from what other church traditions did, as though we might be tainted if we did it too. I suspect that we lacked confidence in our identity and in the core spirituality underlying our practices. Now I sense a different mood. In the past initiatives at Westbury had faced resistance for these kinds of reasons. People objected to singing a few words in Latin or to the use of candles because 'those are things which Roman Catholics do'. However, this time, explaining as we went, and assuring people that these things were intended to supplement rather than replace our core spirituality, people joined in with enthusiasm. Now we could try things and persist with them if we found them helpful and abandon them if not. We tested them by the measure of whether or not they enhanced our worship of God and not by whether they might imply we belonged to some other liturgical tradition.

In the next chapter Paul Fiddes writes about two poles in Christian spirituality. One is that of journey and the other that of stillness. In retrospect I wonder if Westbury had begun to find that traditional Baptist resources fed the side of us focused on journey but did not meet all our needs for stillness. We were able to use resources from other Christian traditions to meet those needs without feeling we had ceased to be 'Baptist'. Baptist spirituality is not some static entity, but is something which is constantly developing. My limited experience is that if congregations are gently and sympathetically given the opportunity to work with other spiritual traditions they will find them helpful and rewarding as they are led to a deeper understanding of God and God's deeds of love for us.

Finally, it occurs to me that different spiritual traditions are sometimes compared to water. Richard Foster's book on different spiritual traditions is called *Streams of living water*. The great liberation theologian Gustavo Gutierrez wrote a book called *Beber en su propio pozo; en el itinerario espiritual de un pueblo*. We might translate 'To drink from your own well; on the spiritual journey of a people'. As a Christian community we continued to drink from our own well, from the stream of Baptist and evangelical spirituality which nurtured us, but we learned also to drink from wells dug and tended by our fellow believers. Our experience was that these fed our need for stillness, helped deepen our spirituality, enhanced our worship of God, inspired our mission and encouraged our continuing journey of discipleship.

Notes

[1] Quoted in David Hay, *Exploring Inner Space. Scientists and Christian Faith*. Revised edition (London: Mowbray, 1987).

[2] John Finney, *Recovering the Past. Celtic and Roman Mission* (London: DLT, 1996), p. 43.

[3] William Stringfellow, *The Politics of Spirituality* (Philadelphia: Westminster Press, 1984) p. 22.

[4] P. Sheldrake, *Spirituality and History: Questions of Interpretation and Method* (London: SPCK, 1995), p. 60.

[5] See Denys Turner, *The Darkness of God. Negativity in Christian Mysticism* (Cambridge: Cambridge University Press), pp. 2-7.

[6] Kenneth Leech, *Spirituality and Pastoral Care* (London: Sheldon, 1986), pp. 36-8.

[7] Augustine, *Ep*. 211.5

[8] Augustine, *Ep*. 211.15

[9] Augustine, *Ep*. 211.11

[10] Augustine, *Ep*. 211.5

[11] Augustine, *Sermo* 355, *De vita et moribus clericorum suorum,* 2.

[12] Augustine, *Sermo* 355.2

[13] The original material from Augustine himself was expanded by two later Rules known as *Regula secunda* and *De vita eremitica ad sororem liber*. Augustine elaborated on his views of monastic life in the treatise entitled *De opere monarchorum*, on the obligation of a monk to devote himself to serious labour.

[14] Rule of St. Benedict, Chapter 2; the text is available in *The Rule of St. Benedict*, transl. by Justin McCann (London: Sheed and Ward, 1976), p. 6.

[15] Benedict quotes from Romans 8:15, and understands 'the spirit of adoption as sons, whereby we cry "Abba, Father"' as being addressed to Christ.

[16] Rule of St. Benedict, Prologue. See McCann, *Rule*, pp. 4, 1.

[17] Rule of St. Benedict, Chapter 5. See McCann, *Rule*, pp. 14-15.

[18] Rule of St. Benedict, Chapter 16. See McCann, *Rule*, p. 28.

[19] These occur in the second rule of 1221, chapters i and xiv. For a reconstruction of the first rule see *The Lives of S. Francis of Assissi by Brother Thomas of Celano*, translated by A.G. Ferrers Howell (London: Methuen, 1908), pp. 108ff.

[20] Third Rule of 1223, ch. 1. The text is available in 'The Rule of the Friars Minor from the Text of 1223' in Constance, Countess de la Warr, translator, *The Writings of St. Francis of Assissi* (London: Burns and Oates, 1907); see p. 28.

[21] Benedict in fact strongly deprecates the 'wandering monks' whom he calls 'gyratory' (Rule, chapter 1).

[22] Third Rule of 1223, ch. 3; de la Warr, *Writings*, p. 30.

[23] According to a letter of Francis; see Letter 3 in de la Warr, *Writings*, p. 71.

[24] Third Rule of 1223, Prologue; de la Warr, *Writings*, p. 28.

[25] Third Rule of 1223, ch. 12.

[26] For the text, see John Morris, S.J., *The Text of the Spiritual Exercises of St. Ignatius, translated from the original Spanish* (London: Burns & Oates, 1880).

[27] See 'Rules To Have the True Sentiment which we ought to have in the Church Militant' (as appended to the Exercises), Third Rule.

[28] These need not be literal weeks, but convenient periods.

[29] 'To Have the True Sentiment', First Rule.

[30] 'To Have the True Sentiment', Thirteenth Rule.

[31] John Smyth, *Principles and Inferences concerning the Visible Church* (1607); printed in W.T. Whitley (ed.), *The Works of John Smyth* (2 volumes; Cambridge: Cambridge University Press, 1915), I, p. 252.

[32] Smyth, *Principles and Inferences*, p. 254.

[33] Smyth, *Principles and Inferences*, II (1609), p. 391.

[34] See *The Confession of Faith of those Churches which are commonly (though falsly) called Anabaptists* (London: printed by Matthew Simmons,

1644), hereafter called the 'London Confession', in William L. Lumpkin, *Baptist Confessions of Faith* (Chicago: Judson Press, 1959); art. XLIV, p. 168.

[35] John Locke, *A Letter Concerning Toleration* (London, 1689), p. 10.

[36] *The London Confession* (1644), Art. XLVII, in Lumpkin, *Baptist Confessions*, pp. 168-9; this is virtually identical to article 38 of *A True Confession* (1596), in Lumpkin, *Baptist Confessions*, p. 94.

[37] e.g. *The London Confession*, Art. XXXIV, in Lumpkin, *Baptist Confessions*, pp. 165-6.

[38] Smyth, *Principles and Inferences*, II, pp. 388-9; 391.

[39] Smyth, *Principles and Inferences*, II, p. 388.

[40] This trend was notably promoted by Theodore Beza. R.T. Kendall, in his *Calvin and English Calvinism*, considers whether the form it took in Puritan England was in accord with Calvin's own theology.

[41] Dudley Fenner, *A briefe treatise upon the first table of the lawe* (Middelburg, 1587), D.1.; cit. Brachlow, *Communion of Saints*, p. 36.

[42] Dietrich Bonhoeffer, *Life Together*. Transl. John W. Doberstein (London: SCM Press, 1972), p. 12.

[43] Bonhoeffer, *Life Together*, pp. 15-18.

[44] The Director of the Northumbria Trust since 1992 has been Roy Searle, a Baptist minister and President of the Baptist Union of Great Britain in 2005-2006.

[45] *Celtic Daily Prayer from the Northumbrian Community* (London: Collins, 2005), p. 10 'The Community Rule'.

[46] *Celtic Daily Prayer*, p. 13.

[47] See the section on the Desert Fathers, *Celtic Daily Prayer*, pp. 424-439.

[48] See the celebration of the Family Shabbat in *Celtic Daily Prayer*, pp. 87-91.

[49] Richard J. Foster, *Celebration of Discipline: the Path to Spiritual Growth. Revised edition* (London: Hodder and Stoughton, 1989).

[50] Robert Warren, *An Affair of the Heart. Encountering God in Prayer and Life*. Second edition (Guildford, Highland, 1999).

[51] www.westburybaptist.org.uk

2
Spirituality as Attentiveness: Stillness and Journey

Paul S. Fiddes

1. Giving attention

In Iris Murdoch's novel, *The Bell*, Paul Greenfield is a guest at a lay Christian community, Imber, which is attached to an enclosed abbey of nuns. He thinks that he is living in the spirit of the community, but fails altogether to notice both the needs and the particular gifts of his wife, Dora. One day she glances at herself in the mirror and 'looked with astonishment at the person who confronted her . . . the person who was there, unknown to Paul. How very much, after all, she existed.'[1] At the beginning of the introduction to this book I remarked that spirituality is a slippery concept, difficult to define and to distinguish from a general concept of religion. Here I want to propose that 'spirituality' is a useful term to express the quality of giving 'attention' to the 'other', a practice in which Murdoch's character Paul is woefully lacking. Because spirituality also indicates a reaching out to what transcends the world of the senses, I want to add that attentiveness to the existence of another is 'spiritual' when it is a means of noticing the reality of an 'infinitely Other'.

Through cultivating attention to persons or to objects which are other than ourselves, we become aware of an infinitely Other—God, who is always giving and disclosing God's self in a loving and costly way. I use the term 'infinitely other' rather than the commonly-employed 'absolutely other', since if God is *absolutely* other it is difficult to see how this God could have any real engagement and relationship with persons occupying space and time. God is, however, *infinitely* other since there is an infinite difference between the uncreated (God) and the created (ourselves). If we focus on this quality of attention in spirituality, then we will have to admit that some Christians may not be very good at fostering 'spirituality', even though they have a real faith in Christ. Their faith has not developed into the capacity to be attentive to Christ, to others to whom Christ relates himself, and to the triune God to whom Christ offers a personal entrance.

To live under the 'rule' or the sway of Christ does not then mean to follow slavishly a set of 'regulations', but to cultivate the habit of attentiveness to the demand that Christ makes upon us in the encounters of everyday life, so that all experience is 'ruled' or measured by the discernment of this demand. To measure other people and things properly, as Hans Urs Von Balthasar suggests, is to notice how they are grounded in the mysterious and beautiful depths of Being itself, as parts in a whole, and it is only possible to measure this beauty because we are first measured by Christ. Christ himself is the true measure or 'rule' of all things; he cannot be measured by an alien standard from outside, but only by himself. His existence and his mission were perfectly in tune with each other, and by giving him the attention due to his measure, we too can be in harmony with his mission.[2] It is possible, on the other hand, that non-Christians might develop a genuine spirituality of being attuned to others, even though they are not directing this attentiveness to Christ. Perhaps this perception begins to validate the general use of the term 'spirituality' today, disconnected from a particular tradition of faith.

'Attentiveness' or attention to what is other than the self, is indeed central to the spiritual quest. The philosopher Emmanuel Levinas, in the wake of the inhumanity of the Holocaust in the twentieth century, has focused on the nature of the self as being radically responsible in the face of the needs and demands of the other person. It was failure to recognize this ethical demand that led to the dehumanizing of the Jewish people. The human self has the urge to dominate others, to reduce them to another version of *itself*, to conform them to the totality of some ideology or world-view. But it will remain imprisoned, merely 'riveted' to itself, until it notices the particular identity of the other. Systems of totality assume that selves are all the same; others are then seen either as extensions of the observing self or as objects to be manipulated for the advantage of the individual or social unit. But this viewpoint does not do justice to others as we meet them for the first time in their strangeness, face to face. They inhabit their own world, and are 'altogether other', with hidden depths of alien existence. The self is thus confronted with the 'infinite', the challenge of the altogether other that shatters our expectations and even holds us hostage by the obligations it imposes.[3] By contrast, as Dora in Murdoch's novel reflects on her love-making with Paul, she finds it 'remote . . . not at all like an encounter with another real human being'.[4]

Levinas has also taken up some of the Jewish spiritual tradition in finding in the face of others a 'trace' of the supremely Other, of the God who has always just 'passed by' as Yahweh passed Moses by with his glory on Mount Sinai.[5] In the end, the demand of the other leads us towards God; but for Levinas this God is always absent, leaving only a trace of himself. As in the experience of Moses on the mountain, others can and must be seen face to face, but not God. A Christian theological response to this account would be to acknowledge that God can indeed often only be known by the 'trace' God leaves, but that this is a sign of a God who is not absent, but rather *hidden* in the world. Hiddenness implies not absence but presence; as Karl Barth puts it, the God who reveals himself veils himself at the same time.[6]

In a whole series of novels, Iris Murdoch depicts characters who learn, or fail to learn, to give attention to what is real around them. This means noticing people as they actually are, rather than as we want them to be for our convenience. It means delighting in all the contingent details of the world, recognizing the 'otherness' of other people and things. Life is thus a long process of 'unselving' in which the self turns its attention to the other, and through this finite other serves an infinite Other. For Murdoch, however, the Other is not a personal God, but the nameless Good which we serve with the hope of no reward ('being good for nothing'). In her novels, Murdoch vividly depicts the feelings of characters who fail to give attention to others, and build a self-enclosed world around themselves. Jake, in her very first novel, sets the tone for a long list of successors when he exclaims, 'I count Finn as an inhabitant of my universe and cannot conceive that he has one containing me.'[7] Murdoch exposes the tragic fact that we all manufacture worlds for ourselves; our minds are the 'sacred and profane love-machines' which she explores in her novel of that title.[8] Other images for the cosmic artifacts that we build and imprison ourselves within are boxes, dark cupboards, cages and eggs.[9]

Art, for Murdoch, is a powerful means of liberating us from these self-made worlds, since it is an object which clearly exists over against us with a reality all its own. It is 'thingy', and by its intense 'otherness' it calls for attention to itself, diverts our attention from ourselves, and prompts a quest for the truth and for the Good. Dora, in *The Bell*, looks at her favourite pictures in the National Gallery, and sees them as 'something real outside herself, which spoke to her kindly and yet in sovereign tones', destroying 'dreary, trance like solipsisms.' Murdoch suggests that reflection upon art is a kind of religious experience, since it

> perhaps provides for many people, in an unreligious age without prayer or sacraments, their clearest experience of something grasped as separate and precious and beneficial and held quietly and unpossessively in the attention. Good art which we love can seem holy and attending to it can be like praying.[10]

This effect is intensified when the work of art is already a religious symbol, whether in visual art or story. In *The Bell* two visitors to the religious community at Imber, Dora and Toby, find the old Abbey bell at the bottom of the lake where it has lain hidden for centuries, and they raise it secretly at night. Gazing on it, Dora feels reverence for it as she had for the portraits in the gallery: 'it was a thing from another world.' The gospel story of the life of Christ, as graven by the medieval artist on the bell, has power to arouse the attention of the observer to reality:

> The squat figures faced her from the sloping surface of the bronze, solid, simple, beautiful, absurd, full to the brim with something which was to the artist not an object of speculation or imagination. These scenes had been more real to him than his childhood and more familiar. He reported them faithfully.[11]

The members of the community at Imber certainly need to have their attention drawn to the truth of the world and other people. Though they are a lay religious community, living in the grounds of an active Abbey, they fail to exercise their spiritual impulses in a way that makes for truth. Both their leaders, in their different ways, fail to notice others as they really are; James is blinded by legalism, and Michael by guilt over a sexual incident in the past. The irony is that Dora, though she recognizes the 'otherness' of the bell and its pictures, intends to abuse it to manipulate the feelings of others; she raises it from water in order to create a 'miracle' which she hopes will shake the community out of its self-righteousness, with its patronizing view of her as 'the penitent wife'. A new bell is to be installed at the Abbey, led there in a procession, veiled in white. She plans to substitute the medieval bell for the modern one: 'Think of the sensation. . . . In this holy community she would play the witch'.[12]

2. Attention, journey and stillness: a threefold connection

I give this example from the novels of Iris Murdoch, not a Christian believer, to show that spirituality as 'attentiveness' covers a large scope of human experience. Christian spirituality, within this spectrum, will be attentiveness to the infinitely Other whom we know, from the revelation in Christ, to be personal and relational. As a *particular* aspect of the religious life, 'spirituality' has thus often been identified with certain practices of prayer, as Murdoch suggests from a non-religious perspective. Meditation, contemplation and 'mysticism' are all associated with spirituality, centring upon practices of 'stillness of the heart' and 'silence of the spirit'.

A place of 'stillness' or 'waiting on God' is indeed one of two central images that need to be drawn into relation with this practice of attentiveness, if we are to do justice to the way that spirituality has developed in the Christian experience through the ages. In stillness we contemplate God, and are helped in doing so by the signs in the world which signify the creator, whether they are signs in other people or in objects of art and nature. The account of experiments in worship in a Baptist church in Bristol, as given in the introductory chapter, recalls the use of such objects as candle flames, banners, projected images of art and even a block of ice as points of quiet contemplation. These are objects that awaken our attention, and their beauty can lead us to the beauty of God. As Barth expresses it, God freely takes objects in the world through which to make God's Word accessible to us, veiling and unveiling God's self at the same moment.[13] As Von Balthasar puts it, the particular 'forms' of things are transformed into beauty by the breaking forth of their inner glory, which is rooted in the glory of the Creator and which catches us up into the communion of God's life.[14]

The other image, which may at first seem to be completely different, is that of a 'journey'. The image of the journey has a central place in writings that are usually labelled as part of the 'spiritual' tradition in western Christianity. St. Bonaventure, for example, called his influential book *The Journey of the Soul into God*. Such a journey was often conceived as taking place in two directions at once: it was both a movement inward to the stillness at the centre of one's being, and an ascent to a divine reality above and beyond the finite world, as if climbing a ladder or a mountain. It was immanent and transcendent at the same time.

In the flow-chart of spiritual dynamics which I hesitantly include at this point (for all illustrations, as Karl Barth pointed out, tend to become idols), the two aspects of journey and stillness face each other across the space of the 'other'. They are two modes of giving attention to the other, whether this be finite others or the infinitely Other. But these two forms of the spiritual life are not separated: the practice of contemplating the other in stillness leads to a journey of experience, and conversely the journey leads to a stillness at the depths of the self. There is a two-way flow between the two poles.

In the mystical tradition there is a dual journey, both 'inward' and 'upwards'at once—*into* the depths of the soul and *up* to the heights of Mount Carmel or Mount Sinai. This journey is commonly thought to end with approaching a source of light which is so bright it can only be experienced by the eyes of the soul as the deepest darkness.[15] The 'spiritual way' is thus often associated with the failure of all words and images before God, an apophatic worship which contradicts all human efforts to reach God through striving or techniques, and in which the presence of God can only be received by the spirit as a gift. It is the silence of the spirit and the end of images, and—as the flow-chart indicates—we can reach this point either by the spiritual journey, or through contemplation. While I have been referring to this place with images of height ('Mount Carmel'), since it coincides with the innerness of the self and anyway is not literally a place it can just as well be depicted at the bottom of the flow-chart, as a dimension of depth.

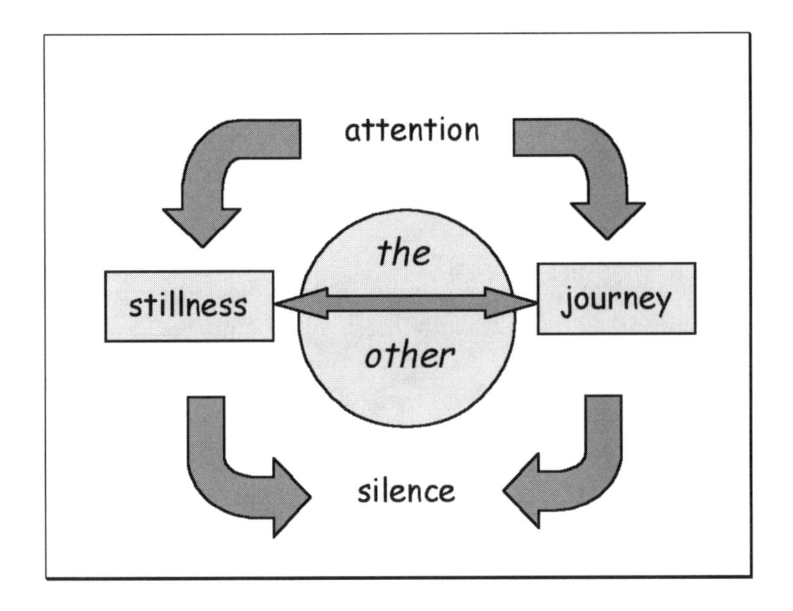

While the tradition represented by this flow-chart has been embodied in particular schools of spirituality with their own practices—for example, the Benedictine and Ignatian spirituality I mention in the introductory chapter—the aspects of 'stillness' of heart and mind and the 'prayer of silence' are distinguishing marks in them all. The flow-chart attempts, then, to summarize a spiritual tradition. It is also, I believe, a useful way of exploring the character of spirituality as attention to the other, even if we do not accept all the implications of the 'silence' as developed in medieval spirituality. I suggest that the related concepts of 'silence' and 'darkness' remain valid as a way of hinting at the overcoming of the split between subject (knower) and object (the known); God cannot be known as an object but only through a participation that eludes all description. I will have more to say about seeing God 'in the darkness' later. We might doubt, however, whether the vision of God promised to the saints will ever be entirely without images (since God is eternally creative and imaginative), and we may hope that when the journey towards the new creation has come to an end, there will be new journeys of discovery to be made eternally.

At first the image of a journey to the centre of the self seems to have the danger of self-centredness, individualism and self-absorption that the quality of attentiveness is meant to counter. But this voyage into the core of the self is in fact a movement into the reality of the Other who—in being known—is necessarily given hospitality within the consciousness. As Thomas Aquinas saw, when any objects or persons in the world are known, they come to occupy space within the observer's mind.[16] This can certainly lead to an attempt at capture and control by the subject, but it can also be a movement of self-giving and *kenosis* in which the self makes room within itself for otherness and difference. So the object known actually awakens the intellect to turn towards it.[17] Hans Urs Von Balthasar builds on Aquinas here by describing the object of knowledge as 'unfurling itself' within the subject; the light of glory breaks from the form of the object contemplated, which discloses itself and invites a mutual opening of the self.[18]

This is why it has been a part of the apophatic 'mystical' tradition in Christianity to find an overlap between a hidden ground of the self and the God who is hidden in light which is so bright it causes a sense of profound darkness. The holding of the known in the knower means that there is a 'place' in which it is not possible to articulate in words the difference between God and the soul. For example, the Lady Julian of Norwich declares that 'I saw no difference between God and our essential being, it seemed to be all God . . .'.[19] It is like, says John of the Cross, the inseparability of the light from the window pane through which it passes.[20] As Denys Turner has pointed out, this is not a simple affirmation that the soul *is* God or that the soul has been totally absorbed into God, but that it is not possible to 'see' or 'name' the difference with our resources of language.[21] The difference is there, but it cannot be named. This is the counterpart, in our experience, to the reality of participating in the triune God who makes room for us in the interweaving movements of the divine relationships—Father, Son and Spirit. In this participation in God there is an infinite difference between the created and the uncreated, but we cannot calculate it or observe it. So God is not an *object* of our desire, where we would possess God, and which would only pander to our possessiveness; rather, we desire in God, *with* the desire of God, and especially with the desire of the Son for the Father.

If we consider the quality of attentiveness to be the essence of spirituality, then the image of the journey can be extended beyond a movement into the depths of oneself; there is a voyage into the lives of others in empathy. In noticing others we imagine what it is like to feel what they feel, and when they have offended us we take the voyage of forgiveness, experiencing vicariously why they said and did what they did. In fact, we share their own journey and become fellow-travellers with them as God does in infinite empathy. The cross of Jesus reveals just how far God has gone on this journey of identification with human beings, into the very depths of his alienated creation.

In summary, I suggest that the term 'spirituality', understood as attentiveness, includes such aspects as a discipline of stillness and receptivity of the mind, an awareness of a mysterious reality of love and justice that transcends what can be empirically tested, and a journey of empathy that flows from such receptivity and awareness. This journey of fellow-feeling into the lives of others will also be a journey of moral transformation for the voyager. For Christian believers, such a kind of spirituality will centre upon a journey into the fellowship of the triune God, through identification with the crucified and risen Jesus. Transformation will be into the image of God manifest in Christ, who is the 'rule' or the measure of all things. But a spiritual journey can still be recognized in those of other faiths and none. This journey into God will involve a journey into the self which does not exclude a journey into the lives of others but embraces it. Attentiveness, stillness and journey interact and interpret each other.

For a Christian, this journey and these relationships happen within a larger journey and a larger set of relations. They happen in God. They take place within the interweaving relations of the triune God, so that the circle of the Other is in fact all embracing, and this is the only reason why there can be a spiritual quest at all. As we pray to the Father, through the Son and in the Spirit, we find ourselves on a journey, involved in a movement of self-giving like that of a father sending forth a son, a movement which the early theologians called 'eternal generation' and which we experience in the mission of God in history. The journey of mission is, we find, marked by deep suffering, like the painful longing of a forsaken son towards a father and of a desolate father towards a lost son. This outward journey is, however, all the while being overlaid by another journey, by a joyful movement like the return of a son to a father in obedience and praise, crying 'Abba, Father'; we can only say 'Father' ourselves because we share in this prayer. Simultaneously, these two movements are interwoven by a third, as we find that they are continually being opened up to new depths of relationship and to new possibilities of the future by a movement that we can only call 'Spirit'. For this third movement the scriptures give us a whole series of impressionistic images—a wind blowing, breath stirring, oil trickling, wings beating, water flowing and fire burning—evoking an activity which disturbs, opens, deepens and provokes. Thus, through our participation, we can identify three distinct movements of speech, emotion and action which are like relationships 'from father to son', 'from son to father' and a movement of 'deepening relations'.[22] Nor can these movements of giving and receiving be restricted to a particular gender; they can also, in appropriate contexts, give rise to feminine images. The experience of our journey may require us to say that we are engaging in a flow of relationships like those originating in a mother (cf. Isa. 49:14-15), especially in experiences of being spiritually nurtured and fed,[23] or like those which characterize the response of a daughter.

Against this background of the spiritual tradition in Christianity in general, I want for the remainder of this paper to explore the way that 'attentiveness' has shown itself in Baptist spirituality in the past and may be cultivated within the life of Baptist Christians and churches today. We may expect to find that the images of 'journey' and 'stillness', or the activities of empathy and contemplation, will be associated with attention to the other and to the infinitely Other. What is distinctive to the Baptist experience is the relative weight given to the aspects of stillness and journey, and the way that they relate within a Baptist way of life and worship, under the rule of Christ. I intend then to examine these aspects of spirituality in the context of five distinctive communal practices: praying, witnessing, singing, communing and reading.

3. Praying

It has been characteristic of Baptist spirituality to cultivate daily private prayer. Rather than the regular 'hours' of the monastic life, classically seven times a day,[24] private prayer has customarily been focused on one period each day, often in the morning. In this section, however, I want to focus on the Baptist practice of leading prayer in public, as one aspect of the spiritual life in community, and here it has been typical to offer either 'extempore' or 'free' prayer. Extempore prayer draws spontaneously on resources of scripture, memory and spiritual experience from within those praying in the very moment that they speak to God. 'Free' prayer may be distinguished from this, as requiring a 'pre-meditation' which involves the preparation of the heart as well as a deliberate reflection on the subjects for prayer. As Isaac Watts defines it, 'free' prayer is 'when we have not the [exact] words of our prayer formed beforehand . . . but we conceive the matter or substance of our address to God'.[25] In the introduction to their once widely-used manual for Baptist ministers, *Orders and Prayers for Church Worship*, Ernest Payne and Stephen Winward suggest that Baptists share the heritage of 'free' prayer with other Free Churches,[26] although this should be qualified by a survey of Baptist churches undertaken by Christopher Ellis in 1996, when those churches which use 'free' prayer explained that two-thirds of their praying was in fact extempore.[27]

Whether prayer is extempore or free, however, its essence is that it is prayer 'from the heart'. As John Bunyan expressed it, sincerity of prayer and purity of heart are essentials of true prayer. When a believer cries 'Father', then 'that one word spoken in faith is better than a thousand prayers, as men call them, written and read, in a formal, cold, lukewarm way'. He goes on to insist that 'prayer, without the heart be in it, is like a sound without life'.[28] In recent years, those leading prayers in Baptist churches have extended the forms of 'free' prayer beyond the limits that Watts laid down, preparing their prayers beforehand by composing them for themselves, and incorporating or adapting written prayers from the great tradition of the church or contemporary resource books (such as those from Iona and the Northumbria Community). They may also provide responsive prayers for the congregation to share in, either in photocopied form or by means of an overhead or video projector. The tradition of free prayer remains, however, in so far as all these materials can be used or combined freely, and can be departed from or varied spontaneously in the moment of praying, unconstrained by any fixed liturgy. The survey conducted by Christopher Ellis is revealing here of Baptist practice: while over 50% of those surveyed reported that prayers were *sometimes* read, only 1% reported that prayers were *usually* 'read from a book'. Whatever the style of pre-composing or preparing prayers, Baptist congregations are in the succession of Bunyan in so far as they expect the prayer of the person leading worship to come from the heart, and to *sound as though* it truly does. The 'cold reading' of a text is not acceptable.

This means that the hearer is being presented not essentially with the reading of a written text (even though texts may be used), but with prayer embodied in a person with a history and with an experience of sin and grace. Bunyan proposes that 'while prayer is making, God is searching the heart, to see from what root and spirit it doth arise.'[29] To a lesser extent, the pray-er's fellow believers are also searching the heart. That is, those hearing are being invited to read a 'person as text'. We may compare here the Apostle Paul's experience of his Christian friends, that they were 'a letter written on my heart, to be known and read by all . . . written not with ink but with the Spirit of the living God' (2 Corinthians 3:3). In modern semiotics, it has become clear that the human body is a network of signs, pointing beyond itself and emptying itself out in the direction of others. The body, which is inseparable from the person, is like a text, communicating a message and speaking a language of signs (indeed, we often speak of 'body language'). Moreover, the embodied person has been shaped by certain written texts, which have exerted such an influence that they are now internalized within the person. Persons, who are already a kind of text to be read, also carry texts within them. Now, Baptist prayer has typically been shaped by the memory of the scripture text. One might say that it is soaked in scripture. Even when it is called 'extempore' it falls into the words of scripture or the patterns of scripture phrases, so that scripture indwells the person praying. In being invited to read the 'text' of a person praying, hearers are thereby being drawn into knowledge of the God who makes God's self known through the text of scripture.

Free prayer thus invites attention to be given to God through attention to another person, rather than to an object (whether a written text or a visual symbol). This is the nature of representative prayer. The nineteenth century Baptist minister William Brock writes of the one praying as representing all those present: 'That prayer, brethren, is offered in your name. Rightly understood, it must be regarded in fact as your own prayer. You do therein acknowledge your insufficiency to think anything as of yourselves, and you gratefully remember that your sufficiency is of God'.[30] Here Brock interestingly suggests that attending to ('regarding') the one praying draws attention to God through the experience of dependency: we are dependent on the one praying and this prompts us to realize that we are dependent on God. Moreover, the one praying is also attentive to the situation and needs of those who are listening: 'that prayer, brethren, is offered in your name'. Dietrich Bonhoeffer, in *Life Together*, likewise stresses the representative nature of prayer in community; all the members gathered should pray for the one praying on their behalf, especially if that person does not feel in the mood to pray: 'everything depends on the fellowship's supporting and praying the brother's prayer with him *as its prayer*'.[31] We should ask ourselves seriously whether we have lost this sense of representative praying in a contemporary practice of public prayer in which everyone is offering their own personal prayers without paying any attention to each other (evidenced by such expressions as 'I just want to thank you', 'I ask you'). Representative prayer calls for attention to the one praying, and so directs attention to God.

Recalling our two poles of spirituality—'journey' and 'stillness'—we might say that the aspect of journey is necessarily more emphasized in free and representative prayer than stillness. Using the objectivity of a written text, often repeated and hallowed by years of use, promotes stillness of heart and mind. The text, with its familiar words, has the 'thinginess' of a work of art, and provides a place for quietness and centring of the spirit, at 'the still point of the turning world'. It enables us to pass beyond the text into contemplation, as we pray 'through' the text, and leave the words and concepts behind. By contrast, paying attention to a person as text is a journey of empathy in which we are drawn into the person's own journey of experience. This may be the person's journey into the world, as he or she leads us in intercession for others who are encountered in daily work or social life. It may be his or her journey through the text of scripture. It may even be a journey deep into the heart of the self in confession or up to the heights of the Mount of Transfiguration in praise, and so we may find that the journey leads us finally into the silence of encounter with God. As we have seen, stillness *or* journey may be means of touching that silence where we find union with the mystery of God, a mystery which is the unfathomable depths of personality.

On these journeys we may meet what is new and suprising to us. It may be that a journey may so expose us (rightly) to the vicissitudes and strains of another person's experience that it is difficult to reach a place of stillness. We are too disturbed by the reality that has been revealed. In contemporary Baptist spirituality, however, whether corporate or private, there has been a rediscovery of attention to objects as a means of contemplation, as indicated above, and this may well include the object of the written text. But we must take care not to lose the element of journeying with others that comes from free and representative praying.

4. Witnessing

Giving witness or testimony has been a characteristic part of Baptist worship, usually—but not only—in evangelistic, baptismal and ordination services. Witness is a kind of spiritual autobiography, given classical written form by Augustine in his *Confessions* and by John Wesley in his *Journal*. These examples have their modern counterpart in the increasing practice of 'journalling', or keeping a regular diary of spiritual growth and discovery, which a number of Baptists have adopted, either on retreat or as a regular practice. But the typical Baptist form of witness in the past has been in a public meeting, and this is given depth in community memory by the historic experience of Baptists and Anabaptists in giving open witness through suffering and death: 'martyrdom', of course, literally means 'witness'. Richard Kidd in the next chapter picks up this thread within the story of Baptists, and its significance for Baptist spirituality. At one time it would have been usual for those wishing to be baptized to offer an account of their faith and experience of Christ to the church meeting, who would then decide whether it was appropriate for them to receive baptism.[32] Rare now in western Europe, something like this practice still exists in Baptist churches in the former eastern Europe.[33]

As with free and representative prayer, witness presents the hearer with the person as a text, as a living human document. We are invited to give attention to the persons witnessing, and their witness is only effective if they themselves are giving attention not to themselves but to the

Other who is the object of their witness. Witness draws attention to the rule of Christ, measuring all human words by the divine Word. As the Baptist theologian James McClendon points out, the costly witness of martyrdom was especially effective in getting the attention of its audience; it engaged not only the believers, but the whole culture which was oppressing them:

> In martyr Christianity, the opponents of the faith are as fully involved as are their victims. Thus the radical work of martyrs cannot be primarily inward-looking—disproving the often-heard charge that baptist practice was 'sectarian' and self-preoccupied. Their focus required disciples to engage the spiritually needy other, to confront the antagonistic other. Martyrdom is of necessity a work of witness.[34]

Witnessing is an invitation to the hearer to share the way that the witness is here and now living in the story of God, and this is only possible because the story of Jesus in scripture gives us the clues to God's story. Giving attention to the witness enables the hearer to 'follow' the story, which links history and theology. McClendon cites the philosopher W.B. Gallie on the dynamics of 'following' a story, which Gallie suggests is analogous to following a game.[35] If an audience is to follow a game—say of football or cricket—then its members must understand the significance of the moves and plays involved. Knowledge of the rules is essential, but not enough. To follow the game properly, an audience needs a commentary by an experienced player, who is able to perceive what the coach, manager and players are 'up to' from a perspective 'inside the game'—why the players have been put in a certain position on the field, why a bowler delivers the ball in a certain way, why the one who strikes the ball puts in a particular direction. McClendon suggest we can draw some implications for following the Christian story. We must know the rules for God's story, in the sense of guidelines for the way that human persons can live in the story; Christ, we may say, discloses this rule of life, as the measure of all things. Then witnesses act as expert commentators, showing us from their experience of inhabiting the story *how* it can be lived within in particular circumstances.

Witness not only gives the hearers clues about living in the story. It also enables the one who hears it to see how God's story interacts with the stories of the contemporary culture. We are surrounded by stories by which people live, and which are also used by those in power to gain control over others. Some stories become dominant, and form an ideology. One example in our present society is the story of redemptive violence, the story—often vividly displayed in films—that justice can be made from the barrel of a gun. Witnesses show how God's story of peace comes into conflict with myths of violence and market-interest. The Hollywood film called *The Witness* (1985)[36] of interest here, in both reinforcing the dominant story of violence, and yet also undermining it at the same time. The film concerns the Amish community, a religious group descended from the Anabaptists of the sixteenth century, who have retained a lifestyle which challenges the modern world. The film begins with a scene in which a young Amish boy, accompanied by his mother, witnesses the murder of a police officer while changing trains. He also identifies another police officer as the murderer. The detective assigned to the case recognizes that the boy is in danger, and so returns with him and his mother to their farm, assumes an Amish identity and clothing, and hides there to evade corrupt officers and protect the boy. The title 'The Witness' is many-sided, referring both to the boy as witness to a murder, but more profoundly to the whole pacifist Amish community as witness to a radically different view of the world from that based on violence and acquisition of technology. The film thus seems to question a prevailing story with the Gospel story, but the story the film itself tells is ambiguous. While the corrupt police officer who finally turns up at the farm is faced down by a crowd of unarmed Amish men, the 'good' police detective quite unnecessarily kills the chief drug-dealer with a shotgun. While the detective has become an admiring observer of the life of the community, it is quite unclear as to whether he has even begun to move towards being a true participant. It is also unclear what kind of ideology the film is attempting to reinforce. Christians who watch the film will be left with uncomfortable questions about the effectiveness of this act of witness, and their own.

When someone is witnessed to, they become spectators of the story, whether in the Bible or in the lives of Christians since the time of scripture. They may be moved by it, as we are moved by a novel or a drama, but being a spectator or audience is not the real point. Those who hear can become players themselves. They cease merely to observe and become participants. Through giving attention to the witnesses they can become disciples, and this is the point of the story, just as watchers of a sport need to know (as Gallie emphasizes) the aim of the game in order to understand it. All this underlines the importance of re-gaining in Baptist spirituality the tradition of witness: not a cliché-ridden account, often repeated and over-worn, of a conversion story far back in the past, but a telling of the way that a person lives here and now in the story of Christ. We need to find fresh expressions of witness, and in the introductory chapter Steve Finamore recounts how his congregation found at least one way of doing so.[37]

It seems that giving attention to the witness of others can, like representative praying, be elucidated more by the image of a spiritual journey than that of a moment of stillness or waiting on God. Attention is being given to the way that the witness has journeyed and is still journeying on, and participation means joining the witness on the journey, as the detective travelled to the farm and into Amish community life. But we can also discern here the interchange between journey and stillness which is hesitantly portrayed in the flow-chart above. There is an aspect of stillness and contemplation when the witness bids those who hear to 'come and see' (John 1:39; 12:21). The desire to 'see' Christ plays a major part in Baptist spirituality, as expressed in such songs as 'Turn your eyes upon Jesus'. The witness invites a seeing of the Christ who *cannot* be seen with the immediacy of physical sight. On the one hand the Gospel of John, in which the theme of 'seeing' the glory of Christ is pervasive, concludes with the promise of Christ addressed to us as future readers of the Gospel: 'blessed are those who have *not seen* me and yet have come to believe' (John 20:29). On the other hand, the witness claims to have seen Christ (1 John 1:1: 'we declare what we have seen with our eyes, the Word of life').[38] There is then an indirect seeing, a seeing mediated through other things and other people so that we have a 'mediated immediacy'. The witness and the hearer together 'see' Christ with imagination as they read the text of scripture, and they learn to see Christ in each other and in other people (1 John 4:12). These are moments of stillness and contemplation on the journey.

Moreover, as the hearer shares in the story of the witness, and so shares in the story of the triune God, there is a kind of 'seeing' which is not observation but participation. There is no object to be literally seen, as God cannot be reduced to an object in the world, but there is an engagement in the movement of the Son towards the Father, in the glorifying of the Father by the Son, which can only be called a vision of God. As we share the journey, we come to see. This is a seeing which is apophatic, which reverses all that we usually call sight; it is nothing less than a seeing in the darkness. St John of the Cross witnesses in his 'Song of the Soul' to sharing in the 'currents' of love between the Father, Son and Spirit, like being plunged in darkness into three flowing streams which merge together. He concludes:

> This spring of living water I desire,
> here in the bread of life *I see entire*
> in dark of night.[39]

Again, the mystic Pseudo-Dionysius bears witness to this kind of contemplation:[40]

> Amid the wholly unsensed and unseen
> they completely fill our sightless minds
> with treasures beyond all beauty . . . .
>
> I pray we could come to this darkness, so far above light! If only we lacked sight and knowledge so as to see, so as to know, unseeing and unknowing what lies beyond all vision and knowledge. For this would be really to see . . . .

5. Singing

In the early days of Baptist life, there was considerable resistance to the singing of congregational hymns, for the same reason as the use of written prayers was rejected; corporate hymns were pre-composed 'forms of prayer', and prayer should flow, it was believed, 'sincerely' from the heart. Among the General Baptists, hymn singing was forbidden until the founding of the New Connexion at the end of the eighteenth century. It seems that the solo singing of a spontaneous song by an individual was permissible, recalling words of scripture from memory, as 'an ordinance flowing from a cheerful heart'. Among Particular Baptists, the corporate singing of metrical psalms was common in the seventeenth century, and towards the end of the century Benjamin Keach pioneered the singing of hymns in his church at Horsleydown, though in the face of some opposition.[41] At first confined to a hymn at the close of the service, to reinforce the message of the sermon, hymn singing rapidly became a staple part of worship, increasing in importance and quantity. Whereas in the eighteenth century it was usual to include two psalms or hymns in the service, by the twentieth century this had increased to four or five. Today, in the movement of 'praise and worship' where the hymn book has disappeared in favour of overhead and video projectors, singing has become the major vehicle of worship; the first part of the service often consists entirely of 'blocks' of songs led by a music group.

Hymns—and until recently the hymn book—function as the 'liturgy' of Baptist and other Free Churches. The earlier objectors were surely correct in identifying the hymn as a 'set' form of prayer, whether sung privately or corporately. Chris Ellis quotes correspondents to the nineteenth-century Baptist paper *The Freeman* as arguing that it was permissible to use read prayers in worship because many hymns were pre-composed forms of prayer.[42] Why then have Baptists, after early hesitations, embraced the singing of hymns while remaining quite largely resistant to a fixed spoken liturgy? A wide freedom of selection among hymns and songs is probably one factor, but the singing of words together in a rhythm may also engender emotion and a feeling of expression 'from the heart', where corporate speaking from a written text has the feel of a 'recitation' to many Baptists. The eighteenth century Baptist John Gill urged congregational singing because different details of the hymn could meet the particular needs of different individuals, so that singing the words of someone else could indeed be 'sincere'.[43] I suggest that there is also a more profound theological reason lying beneath the surface: the pulse and movement of a musical line enables the singer to be attuned to the movements of love and relationship in the life of the triune God about which I have written above.

If singing provokes attention to God, in singing together the participants also need to give attention to each other. It is not possible to sing together 'with one voice' unless the singers are listening to each other and noticing each other. Salvation, as David Ford stresses,[44] is an abundant life, characterized by flourishing, overflowing of joy and 'the polyphony of many voices'. While our atonement depends on substitution and representation by Christ, we can also in a lesser sense exercise these actions towards others—that is, putting ourselves in the place of others in responsibility, love and sacrifice.[45] Ford suggests that flourishing, facing each other, and substituting for each other converge in worship, and are especially focused in singing together.[46] This is salvation, to be transformed as a worshipping self, living with open face before the Creator and fellow creatures. We see that the infinite obligation of the self to others, which Levinas emphasizes, is a matter of sheer joy in the other. Permitting *God* to be for us is a matter of rejoicing, and living before the face of others is similarly an abundant life.[47] All this comes to a focus in singing, where the experience of singing in polyphony with others, each voice contributing to the whole, is one of subjection to others yet without any domination. The hymn or song is destroyed if we merely assert ourselves, our voice drowning others out. And when we use 'I' in a hymn or song, as writers do in the Book of Psalms, we must ensure that it is capacious and not privatized; the 'I' of worship must include other selves who are also sharing in the song.[48] So singing in worship and giving attention to the other are deeply connected.

All this seems to put before us the image of a journey once again. In attending to God, we share in the triune journey of love, the movement of the music helping us to share in the mission of God. We share in the journey of the hymn-writer, in his or her experience of life on which the hymn is drawing. The sequence of thought in a hymn (as distinct from a spiritual 'song'), from first verse to last, also takes us on a journey of discovery in the mind. Many of the themes of hymns are those of journey or pilgrimage, and offer themselves as songs to be sung 'on the way'. These range from the older 'Forth in thy name, O Lord I go', 'Through the night of doubt and sorrow/Onward goes the pilgrim band' and 'O God of Bethel' to the modern 'The journey of life may be easy, may be hard', 'Brother, sister, let me serve you. . . . We are pilgrims on a journey' and 'We are marching in the light of God'.[49] In the last the modern mood of the freedom march fuses with the ancient symbol of pilgrimage. The effect of such hymns and songs should be to prompt us to enter with empathy into each other's journey. But it is perhaps in singing that Baptists also get closest to the other image of spirituality I have suggested—that of stillness before God, or contemplation. This may seem an odd suggestion, as singing involves sound—and often a great deal of volume. But stillness must not be confused with the silence of the spirit towards which it moves, a silence which is also the destination of the spiritual journey (see the flow-chart above). The modern song 'Be still,/ for the presence of the Lord/ the holy one, is here' shows an awareness of this linking of stillness and journey, as it concludes 'Be still,/ for the power of the Lord/ is *moving* in this place'.[50] The familiar words of a hymn or song can act like the familiar words of a set prayer, creating a place where the singer or speaker gets beyond the words and concepts to wait before the face of God.

The use of short songs in modern 'charismatic' worship, repeated several times, can help to foster this quality of stillness of heart. Instead of being led in a sequence of thought through a hymn, a few images circle in the mind and impress a sense of overcoming the flow of time and of a waiting in expectation. In this way, short charismatic lyrics perform the same function as the short acclamations and invocations in the canon of the mass, repeated over again in musical settings: *Kyrie eleison*, *Benedictus*, *Hosanna*, *Agnus Dei*, *Dona nobis pacem*. They assist contemplation, as the longer set pieces in the mass (*Gloria, Credo*) lead us through a narrative just as do more traditional hymns in Baptist worship.

In worship we find that Christ is our new social space, filled to overflowing with the grace and glory of God.[51] This space offers moments of stillness; we live before the many faces which are internalized in our hearts, but we only worship the face of Christ who can be trusted to relate to all other faces. Worship is an inclusive, yet uncrowded, space to be, as singing takes up the whole body into the rhythm and movement of the divine song. Yet this is inseparable from journeying, as singing consists of repetition with variation, and in this way we improvise on the past narrative of salvation. Above all, in the sacraments of baptism and eucharist we are enabled to repeat the substitutionary self of Christ, yet with daring improvisations of the new life. 'Who can tell', asks David Ford, 'what self will be formed year after year through these practices'?[52]

At the same time, singing opens up the borders between ourselves and other human beings. As new voices join in there is an 'edgeless expansion', an overflow in which participants have their boundaries transformed. In the experience of singing, a new *social* space of a community is created. This phenomenon of 'overflow' of the self can be a journey of empathy into the life of another, as closed fences and walls are opened up between selves. In the present mood of 'praise and worship' we need to ask whether the spiritual songs are indeed enabling the participants to stand in stillness before the face of the triune God, and whether they are encouraging a journey into the lives of others—or simply fostering a solipsistic journey into the self.

6. Communing

Baptists have characteristically called the eucharist either 'The Lord's Supper' or 'Communion', and the latter term blends into the 'communion' (or fellowship) that believers enjoy with each other. The participants' awareness of each other, their attention to each other, is thus a central part of the Baptist experience of eucharist. This may be enhanced by the 'giving of the peace', when it is understood as sharing in the blessing which Christ himself gave—and gives—to his disciples after his resurrection: 'Jesus came and stood among them and said to them, "Peace be with you"' (John 20:19). Deliberately noticing each other, our voices can become the means for Christ to speak the essential word of peace. Unfortunately, this moment is more frequently understood as an opportunity for neighbours to 'say hello and get to know each other'.

We can, positively, speak of a sacramental encounter with God in the gathering of disciples of Christ. Paul surely intends this when he uses the phrase 'body of Christ' in an overlapping way of the resurrection body of Christ, the communion bread, and the church. They are all 'body of Christ', not in an absolute identification but because in both bread *and* fellowship we can encounter the risen Christ. Baptist tradition has been quite reliant on the thought of the Reformer Zwingli, who perceived in commenting on 1 Corinthians 10.17, 'We eat bread so that we are made into one bread. . . . What we become by this eating . . . is the body of Christ.'[53]

Correspondingly, the understanding of the 'church meeting' among Baptist churches has been highly sacramental, even though church members would be surprised to hear it described like this. In church meeting the members expect to be able to discern the mind of Christ for them, because he is *embodied* among them through the meeting of their bodies. In the seventeenth century it was common practice for members to hold the church meeting either immediately before or after the Lord's Supper, communion with Christ interacting with communion together. So the church book, which recorded the names of the members, the church covenant and all the decisions taken in the church meeting was sometimes kept in a drawer in the bench behind the Lord's table, or in the 'table pew'. Here is a symbol of the sacramental significance of the coming together of human bodies into the body of Christ—table and church book together.

In this spirituality, however, attention can be entirely diverted to each other and almost none given to the actual elements of bread and wine, whose materiality can be underplayed; typically among Baptists this is shown by using a very small cube of bread and a thimble-size glass of wine—which can even be fruit juice. Such lack of attention is probably influenced by the Reformation conviction (in both Calvin and Zwingli, and affirmed by Baptist writers) that Christ cannot be locally present in the elements, since his risen body is located at the right hand of God in heaven.[54] We may judge that the denial of a localized containment of the body within the bread and wine helps to avoid a substantial or static notion of presence, and allows for a more dynamic kind of presence-as-encounter throughout the whole drama of the Supper. But the unfortunate result of this Reformation theology has been to give little attentiveness to the elements, as material objects that can draw our attention to God and which God can use to communicate God's own presence.

There *has* been attention given to the story which is being remembered, and this is underlined by the Baptist practice of reading the words of institution as a story to be told to the congregation (beginning with 'the tradition which I heard from the Lord I pass on to you . . .' 1 Cor. 11:23). This stands in contrast to the practice of including Paul's words in the prayer of consecration offered to *God* (beginning 'the Lord Jesus on the night when he was betrayed took bread . . . .') as in traditions influenced by the canon of the mass. In attending to the story, the sense of a journey is quite strong. There is a journey of remembrance into the past, and a journey into the future in anticipation of the heavenly feast. Memory (*anamnesis*) brings the past into the present so that we actually participate in the event related, and anticipation brings the future into the present to change it. There is also a journey into the self in self-examination, prompted by the reading of Paul's warning in 1 Corinthians 11:27-32.

Stillness and waiting upon God are, however, less evident in Baptist experience, due to the lack of emphasis on the material objects of bread and wine. Baptist spirituality stands in marked contrast here to that of Catholicism, and even of Lutheranism and Anglicanism. While Baptists will react against any *veneration* of the elements, they may be able to appreciate the act of *contemplation* which is rooted in the strong Catholic sense of 'seeing' the Lord under the earthly species of bread and wine, recognizing that this is not physical sight; we may recall our discussion of spiritual 'seeing' above. The stillness of contemplation has perhaps been undermined by the loss among Baptists of the Reformation doctrine that in sharing in the Supper a believer is raised by the power of the Holy Spirit into the heavenly sanctuary where Christ is, to behold his face.[55]

In the attention to the other and to the infinitely Other created by the Lord's Supper, the image of the journey can surely be reconnected to the stillness which is prompted by attention to the elements. Greater emphasis on seeing, touching and tasting the elements can lead the congregation to notice not just each other, but Christ embodied in each other as the whole body of believers. Taking seriously the way that bread and wine are present to all the senses, and finding that God uses these *material* things to make Christ present will enable us to see the faces and voices of each believer as making up the totality of the body of Christ; we shall be ready to discover that Christ becomes visible and audible in the world through the gathering together of his members.

Here the Calvinistic language of 'spiritual feeding' may no longer be sufficient for us. In the past, among Particular Baptists and some General

Baptists, the idea of 'spiritual eating and drinking', or 'feeding upon Christ crucified' preserved a sense of the real presence of Christ in the Supper and connected communion with Christ in the heavenly sanctuary with the act of consuming the elements of bread and wine on the table. John Gill, for instance, followed in the succession of Calvin when he wrote that: 'to eat of this bread spiritually is no other than the communion of the body of Christ, or a having fellowship with him while feeding on it . . . as bread taken into the mouth and chewed is received into the stomach . . . so Christ being received and fed upon by faith, believers are one body and spirit with him . . . they are one bread.'[56] As this quotation shows, the metaphor of feeding on Christ tends to be individualistic (each believer is 'one bread with Christ') and needs to be supplemented by other images of presence connected with the material object, such as hospitality, pouring, breaking and sharing. The sharing of bread and wine in the eucharist, for instance, might well lead us to find the presence of Christ in a radical *economic* re-distribution of goods in our society.

7. Reading

It may seem odd, in a reflection on Baptist spirituality, to have left the practice of reading scripture to the last. But in fact the centrality of the Bible to the other practices we have explored has been clear: there is a praying which is shaped by words of scripture, a witnessing to the Christ who is known in scripture, a communing through repeating the 'words of institution' in scripture, and singing as a way of improvising on the story of scripture. All these practices illustrate what is often called 'Baptist biblicism', but which is really simply a constant honouring of scripture as carrying authority for the church, regardless of any particular theory of inspiration. The distinctive Baptist practice of reading should, however, be explicitly considered. Other essays in this book, by Nigel Wright and James Gordon, concentrate on the Baptist experience of being 'under the rule of scripture'. Here I want briefly to relate the Baptist practice of reading scripture to the aspects of attention, stillness and journey we have been reviewing.

It is a typical Baptist practice to give attention to scripture. More than any art-object, it is the 'otherness' of scripture that compels attentiveness.

The Baptist theologian John Colwell in speaking of 'the sacramentality of the word' affirms that the reading and preaching of scripture acts as a sacrament, as a means of grace or a vehicle for God's gracious presence;[57] but the phrase may also serve to show that the word draws attention to the God who is present, as do the material objects of bread and wine. For Baptists, however, scripture awakens attention most effectively when it is followed by preaching. Robert Hall, in 1814, thus contrasts the reading of scripture with its proclamation:[58]

> the living voice of a preacher is admirably adapted *to awaken attention*, and to excite an interest, as well as apply the general truths of revelation to the various cases of Christian experience and the regulation of human conduct. When an important subject is presented to an audience, with an ample illustration of its various parts, its practical improvement enforced, and its relation to the conscience and heart insisted upon with seriousness, copiousness, and fervour, it is adapted in the nature of things to produce *a more deep and lasting impression than can usually be expected from reading*.

In earlier years, the reading of the scripture in Baptist congregations was immediately followed by a close exposition of the text read; perhaps this was even interwoven with the reading.[59] Somewhat later in the service there would be the preaching of the word so expounded, in the earliest days by three or four people who would 'prophesy' (teach and exhort) in turn. The encounter with the word was mediated through the expositor and the preacher, so that the word clearly stood over against the congregation with its challenge. Whenever scripture is read in worship, it enables those who hear to participate in the Biblical story of the triune God. When it is expounded it calls the congregation into the journey of God in people's particular circumstances, calling them forward into the goal of the mission of God. By reading, exposition and preaching the word remains 'other', ever new and even strange and shocking in its demand upon the congregation. Since all scripture witnesses to Christ, this demand can be rightly understood as the Christ's own rule. At the same time, mediated through the 'living voice of the preacher', the word of God comes through the journey of human experience of the person preaching. The 'ample illustration' to which Robert Hall refers will have come from personal experience of the preacher or those whom she or he knows.

Of course, scripture is also read privately and devotionally, and Baptists have been enthusiastic about this practice. But they have always seen 'private reading' in the context of congregational reading, where an individual's interpretation is subject to the whole gathering of members together, in order to gain a common mind on the meaning of scripture. In the earliest days, it is probable that the exposition of the scripture immediately after reading it was a corporate activity, the whole congregation conferring on the meaning of the passage before the preaching (or prophesying) took place. The Baptist theologian Steven Harmon has recently suggested that the local congregation, gathered under the rule of Christ, is the Baptist version of the Roman Catholic *magisterium*,[60] judging matters of interpretation. We might add that the preaching of the word is a form of tradition, subordinate to scripture but still the means by which God goes on speaking to the church.

The 'shock' or 'crisis' brought by the word read and preached may be contrasted with the use of scripture in traditions with a fixed liturgy (for instance, Orthodox, Roman Catholic and Anglican). As a matter of fact, there is far more scripture being read in such liturgies than in Baptist worship. Not only are there extensive readings from the Psalms and the Old and New Testaments, where a Baptist service might have only one reading, but the liturgical prayers are largely collections of scripture phrases. Scripture shapes the whole worship. Yet Baptists often have the impression that they are more 'scripture-centred' in their worship than others. The point is that scripture in a more 'Catholic' worship is assimilated into the whole movement of the liturgy. It is internalized within familiar forms of prayer, or read within the sequence of prayers and psalms; much of it will not be alluded to in the sermon or homily which traditionally is appended at the end. Scripture as used in the liturgy is expected to speak for itself, rather than being underlined by the 'living voice of the preacher' and it provides opportunities for stilling the mind. It offers the possibility of living for the period of worship in another atmosphere and ethos than that of the frantic world around. Though the contrast must not be over-stretched, there is some truth in the observation of the Catholic theologian Yves Congar that: 'The Protestants want a Church ceaselessly renewing herself by a dramatic and precarious confrontation with the Word of God. Together with the Fathers we see the Church as the continuous communication, through space and time, of the mystical community born from the Lord's institution and Pentecost'.[61]

Attention to Christ in and through scripture surely needs to take the form of both journey *and* stillness. Despite the Baptist tradition of taking the authority of scripture seriously, there is a curious lack of scripture reading in many Baptist congregations today. The result of singing 'blocks' of spiritual songs may be to edge out any extensive reading of a passage of scripture. The decline in reading may be also due to a lack of willingness to listen to preaching and a loss of confidence in the art of preaching today. Since preaching has been so closely connected to the reading and exposition of scripture, there has been no cultivation of listening to scripture in its own right, and there is little expectation of hearing the Word of God through the very reading of the text. Perhaps a way forward is deliberately to foster a more contemplative approach to scripture. I have already remarked that many people today have found their personal spirituality deepened through using the Ignatian technique of meditating on a passage, situating oneself imaginatively in the story told. This can also be practised in corporate worship, both in leaving a period of reflection after reading scripture (either in silence or with music) and in a narrative style of preaching which places both speaker and hearers in the open space of the text.

8. Conclusion

We have seen that in giving attention to God through attending to persons and to objects in the world, Baptists tend (with the exception of singing) to lay stress on the image of the spiritual journey rather than on a place of stillness where we wait for God. Perhaps this is not surprising given the place of John Bunyan within Baptist affections, stamping the image of 'Pilgrim's Progress' on the tradition of Baptist spirituality. However, the two images have always interacted to some extent in Baptist experience, and I have suggested some new possibilities for their integration today. It is essential to hold them together, for the point of stillness at which it is not possible to tell the difference between the Creator and created cannot be a strictly timeless moment, as it is sometimes conceived to be. As the poet T.S. Eliot perceived, the 'still point of the turning world' cannot be outside time and history, or 'all time is unredeemable'.[62] In giving attention to music, for instance, the moments when time *seems* to stand still are in fact dependent on time, on rhythm and harmonic shifts and modulations; time is not abolished but re-configured. This is an apt analogy for our theme, as we have drawn earlier on the musical metaphor of being 'attuned' to the rule or measure of Christ

The still point must then always be part of a journey, or the development of the self through time. It is a sense of being held within a God who is on journey, always voyaging out of God's self into the desolation of the world. We cannot think that God is trapped within time as we are, our inner selves broken as they are by the flow of past, present and future. But we do not have to think of God entirely outside time either; as the lord of time, God is continually integrating it. The stillness comes, I suggest, not by escape from time but by our working with God in taking up the past, present and future into a wholeness which does not cancel time but heals it. This is only possible by attention to God and to others, measuring all things by the rule of Christ.

Notes

[1] Iris Murdoch, *The Bell* (Harmondsworth: Penguin Books, 1962), p. 45.

[2] Hans Urs Von Balthasar, *The Glory of the Lord. A Theological Aesthetics. I. Seeing the Form*. Trans. E. Leiva-Merikakis (Edinburgh: T. & T. Clark, 1982), pp. 467-9.

[3] Emmanuel Levinas, *Totality and Infinity. An Essay on Exteriority.* Trans. Alphonso Lingis (Pittsburgh: DuQuesne University Press, 1969), pp. 48-52, 79-81.

[4] Murdoch, *The Bell*, p. 182.

[5] Emmanuel Levinas, 'Meaning and Sense' in *Emmanuel Levinas, Basic Philosophical Writings*, ed. A. Peperzak, S. Critchley and R. Bernasconi (Bloomington: Indiana University Press, 1996), pp. 61-4.

[6] Karl Barth, *Church Dogmatics*, trans. & ed. G.W. Bromiley and T.F. Torrance (Edinburgh: T. & T. Clark, 1936-77), I/1, pp. 166-9.

[7] Iris Murdoch, *Under the Net* (Chatto and Windus, London, 1954), pp. 24, 9.

[8] Iris Murdoch, *The Sacred and Profane Love Machine* (1974, repr. Penguin Books, Harmondsworth, 1976).

[9] For the image of boxes, see e.g. *The Book and the Brotherhood* (Chatto and Windus, London, 1987), pp. 377, 595; cupboard, *The Time of the Angels* (Chatto and Windus, London, 1966), p.163; cage, *The Sea, The Sea* (Chatto and Windus, London, 1978), p.442; egg, *The Sacred and Profane Love Machine*, p.107 and *The Time of the Angels* , p. 223.

[10] Iris Murdoch, *The Fire and the Sun. Why Plato Banished the Artists* (Oxford University Press, Oxford, 1977, repr. 1988), pp. 75-6.

[11] Murdoch, *The Bell*, pp. 220, 266.

[12] Murdoch, *The Bell*, pp. 198-9.

[13] Barth, *Church Dogmatics*, I/1, pp. 203-8; II/1, pp.5-10.

[14] Von Balthasar, *The Glory of the Lord,* I, pp. 17-34.

[15] Pseudo-Dionysius, *The Mystical Theology*, in *Complete Works*. Trans. Colm Luibheid. The Classics of Western Spirituality (New York: Paulist Press, 1987), Ch. 1, 1000c-1025b, pp. 136-8.

[16] Thomas Aquinas, *Summa Theologiae* Ia, q.94, a.2; Ia, q.85, a.2; Ia, q.87, a.3.

[17] So Fergus Kerr, *After Aquinas. Versions of Thomism* (Oxford: Blackwell, 2002), pp. 26-8.

[18] Hans Urs Von Balthasar, *Theo-Logic. I. Truth of the World*. Trans. Adrian J. Walker (San Francisco: Ignatius Press, 2000), pp. 62-6.

[19] Julian of Norwich, *Revelations of Divine Love*, trans. E. Spearing (Harmondsworth: Penguin Books, 1998), ch. 54, p. 130. While Julian is usually classified as a 'cataphatic' mystic, it is better to regard all medieval Christian mysticism as an integration of apophatic and cataphatic aspects.

[20] St. John of the Cross, *Ascent of Mount Carmel*, 2.5.7; in *The Complete Works of St. John of the Cross*, trans. E. Allison Peers (London: Burns & Oates, 1964), p. 78.

[21] Denys Turner, *The Darkness of God,* pp. 160-3.

[22] For more elaboration, see Paul S. Fiddes, *Participating in God. A Pastoral Doctrine of the Trinity* (London: Darton, Longman and Todd, 2000), pp. 34-46.

[23] See Michael Jacobs, *Living Illusions. A Psychology of Belief* (London: SPCK, 1993), 68-71.

[24] See Paul F. Bradshaw, *Daily Prayer in the Early Church* (London: SPCK, 1981).

[25] Isaac Watts, *A Guide to Prayer; or, A Free and Rational Account of the Grace and Spirit of Prayer*, in J. Doddridge (ed.), *The Works of the Reverend and Learned Isaac Watts, D.D.* (London: J. Barfield, 1715), pp. 125-7.

[26] Ernest Payne and Stephen Winward (Compilers), *Orders and Prayers for Church Worship*. Fourth edition (London: Baptist Union of Great Britain, 1967), p. xv.

[27] Christopher Ellis, *Gathering. A Theology and Spirituality of Worship in Free Church Tradition* (London: SCM Press, 2004), p. 108.

[28] John Bunyan, *I Will Pray with the Spirit*, in Richard L. Greaves (ed.), *The Doctrine of the Law and Grace Unfolded: the Miscellaneous Words of John Bunyan*. Volume 2 (Oxford: Oxford University Press, 1976), p. 256.

[29] Bunyan, *I Will Pray with the Spirit*, p. 248.

[30] William Brock, *The Behaviour Becoming the House of God* (Norwich: Norfolk and Norwich Association of Baptist Churches, 1845), pp. 13-14.

[31] Bonhoeffer, *Life Together*, pp. 47-8.

[32] See, for example, the account of candidates before a church meeting at St Andrew's Street, Cambridge, in 1761, in K. A. C. Parsons (Ed.), Church Book: St Andrew's Street Baptist Church, Cambridge, 1720-1832 (Baptist Historical Society, London, 1991), pp. 29f.

[33] See the account of preparations for baptism in a Baptist church in Bucharest, Romania, in 1995: in Paul S. Fiddes (ed), *Reflections on the Water. Understanding God and the World through the Baptism of Believers* (Macon GA: Smyth & Helwys Press, 1996), p. 13-15.

[34] James McClendon, Jr. with Nancey Murphy, *Witness. Systematic Theology*. Vol. 3 (Nashville: Abingdon Press, 2000), p. 347.

[35] W.B. Gallie, Philosophy and the Philosophical Understanding (New York: Schocken, 1964), cit. McClendon and Murphy, *Witness*, pp. 352-3.

[36] Released by Paramount in 1885, starring Harrison Ford and Kelly McGillis, and directed by Peter Weir. For an account of this film see Paul S. Fiddes and Anthony J. Clarke: *Flickering Images. Theology and Film in Dialogue* (Macon GA: Smyth & Helwys Press, 2005), pp. 247-50.

[37] See above, p. 16-17.

[38] I am presuming here that the author of 1 John is not the Apostle John who literally saw Jesus, and so that another kind of seeing is being referred to.

[39] *The Poems of St. John of the Cross*, trans. John Frederick Nims. Third Edition (Chicago: University of Chicago Press, 1979), 'Song of the Soul', p. 45.

[40] Pseudo-Dionysius, *The Mystical Theology*, 997B and 1025A, pp. 135, 138.

[41] Opposition notably came from a member of Keach's congregation, Isaac Marlow, in *A Brief Discourse Concerning Singing in the Publick Worship of God in the Gospel Church* (London: 1690). Keach replied with *The Breach Repaired in God's Worship: or Singing Psalms and Hymns and Spiritual Songs Proved to be a Holy Ordinance of Jesus Christ* (London: 1691).

[42] Ellis, *Gathering*, p. 170, citing a letter of 2 October 1868.

[43] John Gill, *Two Discourses: the One on Prayer, the Other on Singing of Psalms* (London: 1751), p. 49.

[44] David F. Ford, *Self and Salvation. Being Transformed* (Cambridge: CUP, 1999).

[45] Ford, *Self and Salvation*, pp. 59-60, 65-70, 72-4.

[46] Ford, *Self and Salvation,* pp. 3-4.

[47] Ford, *Self and Salvation*, pp. 75-7.

[48] Ford, *Self and Salvation*, pp. 122, 132-3.

[49] Authors respectively: Charles Wesley; B.S. Ingemann, trans. S. Baring-Gould; Philip Doddridge; Valerie Collison © 1970 High-Fye Music Ltd; Richard Gillard © 1977 Scripture in Song/Thankyou Music; South African traditional, trans. A. Nyberg © Utryk, Sweden & Iona Community.

[50] Author David Evans © 1986 Thankyou Music.

[51] Ford, *Self and Salvation*, pp. 103-4, 118-19, 129.

[52] Ford, *Self and Salvation*, p. 146.

[53] Zwingli, *Letter to Matthew Alber*, 16 November 1524, trans. in H. Wayne Pipkin, *Huldrych Zwingli. Writings*, Vol. 2 (Allison Park, PA: Pickwick, 1984), 141.

[54] Zwingli, *On the Lord's Supper* (1526), in G.W. Bromiley (trans. & ed.), *Zwingli and Bullinger* (Library of Christian Classics 24; London: SCM Press, 1953), Second Article, pp. 214-22; Calvin, *Institutes*, II, 4, xvii:26, 29-30, pp. 579, 583-6. Baptist agreement can be found in: Thomas Grantham, *Christianismus Primitivus: or, The Ancient Christian Religion* (London: Francis Smith, 1678), 2.2.7, pp. 97-8; Benjamin Keach, *Tropologia. A Key to Open Scripture-Metaphors* (London: Enoch Prosser, 1683), IV, pp. 39-41; John Gill, *Complete Body of Doctrinal and Practical Divinity* (1770). *A New Edition in Two Volumes* (Grand Rapids: Baker Book House, 1978; London: 1795 repr. 1839), II, bk. 4, p. 651.

[55] Calvin, *Institutes*, II, 4, xvii:16, p. 569.

[56] Gill, *Body of Divinity*, II, bk. 4, p. 655.

[57] John E. Colwell, *Promise and Presence. An Exploration of Sacramental Theology* (Carlisle: Paternoster, 2005), pp. 88-105.

[58] Robert Hall, *Hearing the Word*. Circular Letter of the Northamptonshire Baptist Association (Kettering: 1814) pp. 3-4. Cited in Ellis, *Gathering*, p. 145. My italics.

[59] Ellis, *Gathering*, pp. 127-8

[60] Steven Harmon, *Towards Baptist Catholicity. Essays on Tradition and the Baptist Vision* (Carlisle: Paternoster, 2006), pp. 63-9.

[61] Yves Congar in Josef R. Geiselmann, *The Meaning of Tradition* (New York: Herder and Herder, 1966), pp. 104-5. I am indebted to my colleague Timothy George for drawing my attention to this quotation.

[62] T.S. Eliot, 'Burnt Norton', *Four Quartets*, in *The Complete Poems and Plays of T.S. Eliot* (London: Faber and Faber, 1969), pp. 175, 171.

3
Spirituality in Suffering: a Defining Experience

Richard Kidd

1. Giving attention to experiences of suffering

As a group of writers, early on we listed the range of themes which might be covered in a book exploring Baptist spiritualities. As soon as we began to do this, there was little doubt that it would be necessary to deal at some length with the very particular role that suffering and extreme adversity have played in our Baptist story. Given the dramatic and acutely painful way that Baptists emerged as a distinguishable movement in Britain and more widely in Europe in the seventeenth century, my own hunch was that it should be possible to map those often agonizing experiences onto at least some of the distinctives that have stayed with us throughout our longer history. I thought that those beginnings must have somehow encoded themselves onto what everyone these days seems to be calling 'our Baptist DNA'. This chapter suggests that the hunch was right, and it begins to offer some of the evidence that might support it.

My aim is for this chapter to have a clear logical continuity with some of the tracks which Paul Fiddes lays in the preceding chapter. Like him, I will be looking at some of the distinctive forms that praying, witnessing, singing, communing and reading scripture have taken amongst us, though in my chapter the focus will specifically be on experiences of suffering, both in relation to others generally and to the infinite Other in particular. In the spirituality of attentiveness, my concern is for attention to experiences of suffering.

The impact that these experiences have on us today, not least on myself, takes a variety of forms. I am particularly aware that, as a Baptist pastor and as a theological educator privileged to travel and meet with some outstanding Christian disciples around the world, in places where too often the toll of human suffering has been and is unacceptably high, the opportunity to give attention to others in contexts of extreme adversity has turned out to be a very significant influence on my own faith journey. I hesitate even as I say this, because it would be utterly offensive and totally inappropriate for anyone to advocate living off some kind of pastoral voyeurism in which the primary motive for involvement with others reveals itself in the end to be no more than self-gratification. I can only hope that no one will rush to interpret what I write in that way. It just seems to me that the possibility of being in places where it is possible to give dedicated attention to another who suffers, is itself a gift of grace, an extraordinarily privileged spin-off from engagement with the world and its many pains.

What has inspired me most is that so many of those I have met face to face, who have lived with deep suffering, also turn out to be people who, in turn, are finding their own inspiration and extraordinary strength through their dedicated attention to the infinite Other, especially as they see it played out in the story of suffering worked out in God's Christ. What this does, then, is to push me to turn my own attention more fully to Christ myself, so that I too can feed directly on the grace which God offers to me through him.

Now, at first sight, this might seem to be a spiritual dynamic which we share in common with many other Christians, and therefore not especially Baptist at all—and in part this must be true. But I think it is possible to contrast what I have been describing from my own experience as a Baptist with what I find in a number of other movements from within the variety of Christian traditions. In those cases the starting point of the faith-building process is not so specifically the suffering of fellow-believers and other human companions, but takes a quite different form, with more 'abstracted' attention to the specific suffering of Jesus, viewed as the man from Nazareth dying on a cross. I am thinking, for example, of the traditions which call attention, as the starting focus, to his wounded and bleeding body. This is probably best exemplified in devotion to the Sacred Heart of Jesus (especially in its more popular and, in the view of many, gruesome forms), or indeed any of those traditions, many evangelical, which specially parade the intensity of Jesus' pain in his experience of dying on the cross as the primary witness which calls us to gospel faith. In an extreme and I think distorted form, cults of martyrdom sometimes actually encourage people actively to embrace, even seek out, physical suffering as a pathway to deepening the faith journey.

Perhaps I am painting the contrast too starkly. Of course many Baptists are eloquent preachers of the sacrificial demonstration of God's love in the crucified Christ. We might even identify our own equivalent to devotion to the Sacred Heart, especially in our much-loved hymns: 'See from his head, his hands and feet/ Sorrow and love (or is it blood?) flow mingled down.' All I am suggesting is that for a people whose origins began with intense experiences of personal suffering, uninvited for themselves or their companions whose pains they had also to attend, the inner dynamic and balance of the process takes on a different form. In this instance, attention to others, either their contemporaries or their ancestors, all actual faith companions, becomes a distinctive energy for the sustaining of faith and growing in it. In the end, whether starting from the suffering of Christ or his disciples, the ultimate (infinite) source of inspiration is God, working by his Spirit—but perhaps there is a recognizable difference of dynamic. This subtle distinction might not be unrelated to the subtly different—and at best complementary—emphases in Anselmian and Abelardian approaches to the activity of God in atonement. My suggestion here is that giving significant attention to others, companion disciples, especially in the extremes of their suffering, tips more towards Abelard, finding its energy in an appeal of love, moving the heart in an empathetic response, than it does to Anselm with his more contractual (earlier I used the word 'abstracted') approach to inspiration and faith.

In a first attempt to flesh this out, I shall now visit, though only very briefly, some of the trails which were laid by our Baptist parents around the time of our first emergence in the turbulent years of the early seventeenth century. We need to try and feel for something of the context and the energy of those days. I shall then make a massive leap to the late twentieth century, looking for identifiable parallel trails still to be seen in our own time. My guess is that similar explorations in the intervening centuries would in fact produce their own not dissimilar results.

2. Beginning with Baptists in the seventeenth century

Giving attention, then, to some of our most famous Baptist parents in faith—John Smyth, Thomas Helwys, William Kiffin, Thomas Lambe, Agnes Beaumont, women and men of peculiar faith—we find a particular kind of passion which shapes their discipleship and the spirituality which sustains it. There is from the start a deep love for scripture and a particular kind of praying, both 'free prayer', as Paul Fiddes named it in the previous chapter, and genuinely 'extempore' prayer too, which arises directly out of living in precarious and potentially threatening contexts. The experience of pain forces, as it were, what others also call the 'prayer of the heart', with its self-authenticating immediacy. Again this is not exclusively the domain of Baptist spirituality; the Roman Catholic Thomas Merton, for instance, extolling the virtues of contemplative prayer, also emphasizes 'prayer of the heart'[1] as crucial for him in the authenticity demanded by a search for inner silence—something I increasingly see as a dynamic equivalent of what many Baptists know when they offer themselves in free and extempore prayer. What both Baptist and Catholic versions of this prayer from the heart have in common is their rejection of superficiality, mere formality, mere repetition of any formula of words.

There is also a deeply moving earthiness about the enthusiastic endeavours of many of our early Baptist preachers, ' "mechanic preachers", untaught, sometimes actually illiterate',[2] displaying profound spiritual intelligence, something evidently fuelled by the Spirit of God, who equipped them 'beyond their station' and actually made them seem a threat even to educated incumbents in the official church. So, in 1645 Thomas Lambe and one of his fellow preachers was, 'arrested under a recent ordinance of parliament forbidding preaching by those not ordained as ministers';[3] and not merely arrested but made to suffer grievously for their obedience to God.

In this section, I am largely dipping into Barrie White's *The English Baptists of the Seventeenth Century* and extracting a common theme. He tells, for example, the story of Edward Barber, a General Baptist and merchant taylor of Threadneadle Street, London, who by 1641 had suffered imprisonment in Newgate gaol for his opposition to infant baptism and to the demand for the payment of tithes. Barber had argued that 'no man ought to be forced in matters of religion, the Gospel being spiritual and requireth only spiritual worshippers like to itself: which cannot be made so but by the Word and Spirit of God, which breatheth where and when it listeth and not where and when men's laws and statutes pleaseth which may make hypocrites but not true Christians'.[4] That is a very good example of the demand for immediacy, authenticity, a 'from the heartness', which gives a very special shape to Baptist spirituality—and is so threatening to others who do not recognize its equivalent in their own hearts.

Through his experience Barber also illustrates very clearly for us how it is attention to Christ, and especially to his sufferings, which galvanizes a commitment to live in this radical way. Writing about those who were to be appointed messengers, he specifically instructs them that they are not to flee persecution but to 'lay down their lives for the publishing and defence of the Gospel if God call them to it', for they must remember that they 'do represent the very presence and person of Jesus Christ.'[5]

As the century progressed the message became ever more clear: it was simply not acceptable in conscience to defer to any authority as higher than that of Christ—and the toll on whole communities for such resolute dissent was extremely heavy. Barrie White quotes Margaret Spurford's account of the 'alienation from their natural communities experienced by dissenting villagers in Cambridgeshire in the seventeenth century' and adds that 'there can be no doubt that this would be felt all over the country.'[6] Absolute separation from the Church of England had a high price attached to it, and was something which bound dissenting communities together in a very special way. The implications for individuals, church members perhaps even more than ministers, were also often far reaching; they included a boycotting in business affairs, the inability to act in legal matters, and ultimately the threat of imprisonment.

Not that any of this should be read as indicative of a peculiar awkwardness of spirit. In the *Humble Representation and Vindication* (1654), in which a number of messengers and elders made their response to the establishment of Cromwell's protectorate, they emphasized their full willingness to obey 'the powers that are in present being' except, of course, in matters of religion, when in obedience to God they recognized that they must be prepared 'either patiently to suffer or humbly to entreat favour.'[7]

Indeed, the motif of patiently suffering the consequences of disobedience, in the name of conscience, without any violent resistance is a recurrent theme. The outcome after the Restoration of monarchy in the early 1660s was that large numbers of ministers—according to Barrie White more than a thousand—formerly in the Church of England were unable to make the declarations of loyalty required for them to retain their livings.

All of this fosters a particular slant on spirituality. We find that when in the 1660s some of the leaders of the Abingdon Association, then in Reading gaol for refusing to take oaths they thought unlawful, wrote about the congregations from which they had been removed, they reported that they 'are exceedingly cheerful, and a very lively spirit of faith and prayer is amongst them and their meetings rather increaseth than otherwise.'[8] Barrie White writes, 'Amazingly, the life of congregations was carried on . . . at its best it meant that kind of care for one another whereby the members helped each other to keep what they believed to be a high and holy obedience to Christ.'[9]

Alongside and out of these experiences there are several early examples of attempts to formulate a theology of suffering fitting for the circumstances of the day, and appropriate to those suffering persecution. Barrie White tells the story of Abraham Cheare, pastor of the Calvinistic Baptist church in Plymouth who, in August 1663 wrote to a friend, recently released from prison, of how important it was 'to get the heart established in grace, drawn into a more substantial and experimental communion with Jesus Christ', even asserting that those who would seek such a deeper experience 'may have more advantage from the retirement of a nasty prison, than . . . from being left to walk in a large place.' To another friend who had recently been arrested at a meeting for worship, he wrote telling him of his 'real opportunity to exalt Jesus Christ in suffering for his name's sake.'[10]

Much less well documented, there is, of course, a highly significant story to be told about the experiences of women in these formative years. One which has been recorded is the story of Agnes Beaumont, born in 1652 and a member of the Bedford church from 1672, at that time in the pastoral care of John Bunyan. As Barrie White recounts, Agnes Beaumont, seemingly through no fault of her own, other than enthusiastic commitment to a dissenting faith, found herself the object of scurrilous accusations against her character—no doubt reinforced in its venom on the grounds of her radical faith in defying a patriarchal society. Her experiences are preserved in a manuscript published much later, in 1760. Raymond Brown[11] identifies four key strands in her evident spirituality, strands which very much reflect the mood of the times: the sovereignty of God, the reality of grace, the inevitability of suffering, and the comfort of scripture—and I am sure it would be proper to add, the comfort of prayer.

Agnes Beaumont's experience may well be used to describe the faith journey of many, both women and men, whose stories form the origins of our Baptist movement. The reality of grace, mediated through prayer and scripture, in their encounter with suffering is surely central, and it is these characteristics which, it seems, provide a loose but significant template for a lasting movement which, whilst retaining basic continuity, will undergo many twists and turns through the coming centuries.

3. Attending to Baptist experiences of suffering today

It might seem a little extreme to leap from Agnes Beaumont to some explorations of Baptists in the late twentieth and early twenty-first centuries—but it is precisely this leap which will test out whether there is any credibility in identifying the characteristics that I have begun to identify as in any way lasting marks of our movement.

I begin by tapping into my own experience of some contemporary Baptist communities in Africa and Central America. Through a number of visits to black Baptist communities in South Africa, I met an energetic and resilient spirituality which took me beyond any frames of reference I had previously known. Three events come to mind, which I think illustrate well parallels between Baptist origins and more recent settings of intense conflict and suffering.

In the first, I recall visiting a black family in a rural community north of Johannesburg. The homestead was substantial but basic. I was travelling as the companion of an experienced local pastor, who introduced me to the 'father' of the house, and we began to converse at first alone in the main living space of the home. We spoke together, in one sense quite formally but, in another sense, already in a deep and engaged way. In response to my rather naïve questions I began to hear the stories of desperately hard lives, struggles caused by severe deprivation, and occasions of significant loss and profound suffering. At a subtle cue which I failed even to notice, the wider family began to enter the room; it seemed as if they had been waiting patiently until the formalities were complete. Before long the room was full—four generations together, men and women, young and old, welcoming this strange guest from a world beyond their horizon. I was asked if I would pray for them, which I did—though it felt to me even at the time that I did so with a certain banality hardly worthy of the occasion. And then . . . and then they began to sing. At first it was tentative, but soon it began to grow to a fullness until this dozen and a half voices were searching out some of the richest harmonies I have ever heard in my life, before or since. And there were the words: 'After all the Lord has done for me, I will never turn away any more.' It was profoundly moving, and seemed to bring to the surface some of the deep pains of lives marked by a passionate identification with Christ.

The second event happened late one afternoon in the tiny classroom which in those days we called the Baptist Convention College. It was February in the southern hemisphere and a wave of intense cold and damp came and settled in for several days. Many Africans seem to find these conditions very difficult indeed, not least because they do not have sufficient clothes to protect themselves at this season of the year. Gradually an air of despair had come over the class—not something I have come to expect when I am the teacher! Then, quite suddenly, seemingly unprompted, and certainly without reference to me, one of the women students got up from her seat, moved her chair to one side, and began to sing. Others were quick to follow and, before I could really interpret what was happening, all the chairs were back to the wall and the class was moving to the rhythms of beautiful music, in a circle around the tables. As in the family home, in the intensity of their engagement with the task of singing, there was that searching for harmonies, rich harmonics which filled the room with something strangely energizing and immensely beautiful. One man, normally very silent in the context of theological discourse, was feeling passionately for the deepest notes, providing a kind of harmonic drone way below all the other voices. And as they sang, they all came to life. All the oppression of weather, my teaching, the tiredness late in the day, all cast aside and soon we were all lifted and vitalized as the Spirit of God picked us up through the music. It reminded me of another testimony I had heard elsewhere, far away in a first world community in North America, from oppressed people who spoke of 'singing their way back into hope'. It seemed to me a profound illustration of the way that suffering people evolve special kinds of spirituality to meet their needs. It fills out, I think, what was written about giving attention to each other and God in singing in the previous chapter.

The final example was not particular to one occasion alone, but illustrates a common feature of much corporate worship in African communities—others who have travelled in these parts will know it well. It might be common, but I still remember acutely my own first encounter with it. I had been asked to lead worship in a township congregation and, following my own common practice, came to a point in the service at which I said the familiar words, 'Let us pray'. Suddenly it felt as if we were in danger of losing the roof. I thought I had been inviting people to assume a quiet and respectful posture as I, pastor for the day, led them in prayer. Not a bit of it. Within seconds many were out of their seats and everyone was praying aloud, each praying their own prayers, some quietly, others with passionate energy as they punched the air pleading with God for a transformation of the world, both theirs and the wider world beyond. In my innocence I thought it all wildly chaotic and could not imagine how order would ever be regained. But sure enough, as simply as it had started, everyone seemed to know when their prayers were complete, quietness fell, and people looked back to me to offer the next word. In retrospect I think I was tasting a little of the intensity of prayer as it must be in the vaults of heaven where saints in rainbow colours plead with God for the causes of the world—and I gained another glimpse of what it looks like when suffering people pour their hearts out in the presence of God.

So what do I now make of these three moments of song and prayer? Once over the initial shock which comes to a typically reserved European, I began to see and to feel something of the sheer power of spiritualities born out of suffering. Here were some of today's Baptists, ordinary people sharing in common with each other a desperation for justice and the basic provisions of life. But counter to another of my European expectations, their hardship did not breed cynicism or discontent, but a passionate spirituality, nothing less than a sharing in the sufferings of Christ; in one case, in the classroom, it was quite literally a *perichoresis*, that word often reserved for the dance which is shared by the persons of the holy Trinity in the eternity of God's heaven. There in Africa, I was experiencing the birthing of another Baptist movement whose spirituality will long be moved by the pain of its origins, even when noone remains who can remember the particular pains of those formative days.

Across the world in El Salvador, Central America, I saw many parallels, though everything as we might expect wonderfully tailored to the particularity of a different context. Baptists in El Salvador are very much a minority presence alongside a massive Roman Catholic majority. For many, however, this has been far from a threatening experience, and solidarity in suffering under successive government regimes and a devastating period of civil war has fostered some remarkable ecumenical relationships. This is the only place I have found in the world where, at a celebration of The Lord's Supper which was otherwise thoroughly 'Baptist' in ethos, the table carried alongside bread and wine pictures of recent 'martyrs', Baptist martyrs, from the conflict of civil war.

It seems that in the intensity of this context many Baptists have been able to cross more freely the ecumenical divides which elsewhere have robbed Baptists of much of the richness of our wider Christian inheritance. Baptists too have found great strength by giving attention to the extraordinary lives of some of the Roman Catholic Christians who have provided such a sacrificial and prophetic presence in El Salvador. Baptists alongside many of their catholic companions in poor and rural communities have drawn massively on the martyr story of Oscar Romero, sharing in large numbers (from their small number) in the anniversary celebrations of his death in 1980. They have also felt free to be enriched by the profound spiritual contribution of El Salvador's world-renowned theologian, Jon Sobrino, teacher at the University of Central America in San Salvador. For me, like many others, it was a very significant life-moment to visit him and the rose garden at the UCA with its memorial to the martyrdom of his six Jesuit colleagues and their two housekeepers, Julia Ramos and her daughter Celina. Most stunning of all, however, was to be taken to the small museum where the memory of that terrible night is preserved as lasting witness to God's grace and the courage of faith which

God inspires. One of the most extraordinary exhibits is a copy of a Spanish translation of Jürgen Moltmann's book *The Crucified God*. By some strange twist of events, now symbolically powerful, when one of those murdered, Juan Ramon-Moreno, was dragged into an inside room, a copy of *The Crucified God* fell from the bookcase and began to soak up his blood.

Here it is, happening all over again. I, along with other Baptists, have found peculiar strength in giving our attention to this extreme experience of human suffering. For me it has contributed to my own strivings to be the best college Principal I could manage to be in my own relatively calm and bloodless context; but for Baptist sisters and brothers in El Salvador, it has continued to provide courage to survive and indeed to triumph in their own circumstances of often hopeless affliction. And attention to the human person, the other, leads to a focusing of attention on the infinite Other, the God whom Moltmann declares to be uniquely present in the crucified one.[12] Once again, I am finding in this Latin American spirituality echoes of the themes which I began to identify as significant to early Baptists in seventeenth-century Britain, most clearly in the deep strength accessible to us all in solidarity with the suffering Jesus. This is a message which I continue desperately to need in my own context, if I am to shun complacency and begin to rediscover some of my deepest roots in our offshoot of God's family.

In El Salvador, of course, I did not find exactly the same patterns of expression that I found in South Africa; the mood was altogether more restrained. This is inevitable in a culture much more deeply shaped over many more years by the influence of Roman Catholic missionary involvement. What was striking, however, was the way that these differences were put into their real perspective by over-arching similarities born out of the experience of suffering. In both contexts, individuals of outstanding stature have been hugely significant—and I could appeal to stories of Desmond Tutu in South Africa as easily as I can of Romero in El Salvador.

But I do not need to visit other continents to find similar manifestations of these motifs in recent Baptist experience—I can find them here in Europe too. One important context which comes to mind is that of the Evangelical Baptist Church of Georgia, known to many Baptists around the world through the remarkable work and personal testimony of Bishop Malkhaz Songulashvili.[13] The more I learn about his story and that of the Baptist community in Georgia, the more I am inspired for my own faith journey. The story of bitter conflict with competing authorities, both church and state, is deeply moving. The way that Baptists have responded to this, often with that quality, identified earlier in other Baptist stories, of patiently suffering the consequences of their own integrity, is impressive. A key moment came quite recently when Bishop Malkhaz offered forgiveness and reconciliation in open court to the defrocked Orthodox priest (disowned by his own church) who had been responsible for inciting mobs to break up services, burn churches and attack Baptist believers. Moreover, like Salvadorian Baptists, Georgian Baptists have found it possible to cross ecumenical divides which others would hesitate even to approach. This is made concrete in the exploration of icons—most famously in the Baptist icon school—careful attention to ancient liturgical forms and, symbolically, in the use of distinctive clerical dress which taps deep into the expectations of a long-established culture. Again, it might have been expected that opposition, even violence, could breed cynicism and even despair; but the message which comes across as an inspiration to others around the world is one of a widened openness to hope, and stronger vitality in God.

4. Baptist theological reflection on suffering

A significant place for exploring the motifs of suffering, and their implications for spirituality, has been our Baptist College in Oxford, Regent's Park College. After glimpses of Baptist life in Southern Africa, Central America and the former Eastern Europe you might be forgiven if you do not immediately think of turning to what many assume is the rarified atmosphere of the University of Oxford in search of some of the most incisive theological reflection on the experience of human suffering in recent times; but failure to do so would be to miss a rich part of our inheritance. For the purposes of this account, I begin with the work of Henry Wheeler Robinson, Principal of Regent's Park College, first in London then in Oxford, from 1920 to 1942. Robinson's specialism was Old Testament, and he is well known for his scholarly contribution to that field. Robinson's writing, however, is always so much more than the analytical work of a linguistic and textual critic; he writes out of a deep passion for the Christian faith and its relevance at every level of human experience. This is clearly exemplified in the three monographs, later gathered under the summary title *The Cross in the Old Testament*, published in 1951. These comprise *The Cross in Job* (1916), *The Cross of the Servant* (1926) and *The Cross of Jeremiah* (1925).

Robinson's search for the cross in the Old Testament deserves careful attention. This is no trivial attempt to make literalistic connections between Old and New Testament texts. Much more profoundly, it is a counterpoint to a long-established hermeneutical method—namely, that of letting the Christ of the New Testament become the moral and theological canon, the 'measure', by which to judge the lasting significance of Old Testament ways of thinking about God's activity in the world. It is exegesis under the 'rule' of Christ. In Robinson's hands it becomes a way of mapping some of the complex pathways by which New Testament writers were able to gather and build on remarkable and pioneering insights from their Hebrew forebears. It also follows the Baptist dynamic I have identified: beginning from the suffering of human servants of God, especially the prophets (and notably Hosea and Jeremiah), our eyes are then turned to the pain of God in Christ..

It is in *The Cross of the Servant* that Robinson makes some his boldest claims to fresh insight. The first two sections of the book rehearse much of the work expected of Old Testament scholars, exploring the person of the Servant in the book of Isaiah and the historical significance of his story. Robinson then moves, however, to make a number of links between the Testaments. He explores the way that the portrait of the Servant might be said to shape the consciousness of Jesus as we have received an understanding of it through the New Testament. Then, significantly, he goes on to consider the way that this has in turn shaped the corporate consciousness of the church. Finally, he follows the track from human suffering to divine, clearing new and important ground. He begins to spell out his own convictions about the implications for our lasting Christian understanding of God, and God's relationship to a suffering world. On the very last page, he writes:

> In spite of much Church doctrine, an impassible God is as impossible as a docetic Christ. In the last resort, the sacrifice is God's, and corporate personality attains its supreme achievement in the sacrificial realization of the kinship of man and God. The final appeal of grace is in the suffering God, as the final depth of sin is the churlishness that scorns such grace. We may see in the Servant of Yahweh the portrait not only of Jesus of Nazareth, but of the Eternal God in His most salient attribute of covenantal and sacrificial suffering.[14]

This is bold indeed. Today we live with the idea of a suffering God with much greater ease, thanks to the influence of writers such as Jürgen Moltmann, quoted above, and a host of modern poets and hymn-writers[15] who make such a theme seem commonplace. But back in 1926, these were words which would arouse to fierce objection the more comfortably orthodox, who assumed that all such ideas belong with the early Christian heresy (so-called) of patripassianism.

This was, of course, the kind of radicalism that could have been anticipated from the author of the ground-breaking *The Christian Doctrine of Man*, first published back in 1911. It was to reach new heights, however, with a book published around the outbreak of the Second World War in 1940, under the title *Suffering Human and Divine*. In this work, Robinson elaborates the arguments rehearsed many years before, now focused in a word of prophetic significance to the particular context of Europe at that critical moment. As in earlier writings, the argument develops with meticulous rigour from accepted scholarship on the interpretation of biblical texts, through to chapters in more apologetic mode which increasingly focus attention on the relationship between God and the suffering of God's creation. A chapter on 'The Suffering of God' challenges the idea that it is possible to do any justice to the idea of atonement without taking God's self-sacrificial participation in the process of human transformation with the utmost seriousness; what we see in the suffering of Jesus is but a 'window' into the divine heart.[16] This is a complex argument, and it is not possible to do it full justice in a brief summary like the one given here. It demands, for example, a careful re-evaluation of how we understand the relationship between God and time, Robinson's preference being for a phrase like 'time in God' rather than 'God in (or out of) time'.

In the two powerful chapters which follow, Robinson argues from his basic thesis, 'that there is no valid philosophical or theological objections against the doctrine that God suffers, and that the genuinely Christian conception of God in fact requires that, in some sense, he should be a suffering God',[17] through to a new understanding of the experience of suffering in the life of the world and of the Christian community. In so doing, he appeals for a fresh grasp of the relationship between 'objective' and 'subjective' dimensions of our concepts of atonement, a new bringing together of Anselmian and Abelardian insights. The purpose of his argument, however, is to effect a transformation in the way that committed believers might understand and interpret the experience of suffering in which they themselves are caught at the outbreak of war in Europe. Robinson thus writes about the close connection between our suffering and God's own suffering:

> If that be true, our human history acquires a new meaning. It is no longer the record of a questionable progress to the dubious goal of human perfection, under the shadow of a slow fading out of life or a cataclysmic end to it—a goal which, even if achievable, would still leave unanswered the problem of the suffering of countless generations which have been but scaffolding to the building of the last generation of all. History now becomes the record of man's privilege to share, by his very sufferings, in the redemptive work of God, through which even the record of history with all its sin and shame may be transformed into the record of God's grace. We must indeed go on working for the betterment of man on earth, physical and spiritual and moral. That is both the test and the means of the inner growth into fellowship with God.[18]

So we see that, in Robinson's view, this is not merely a shift of ideas, a rearrangement of mental constructs for the satisfaction of the intellect. Rather, it is a way of understanding which can reshape the active engagement of Christian disciples in work towards the transformation of the world. This is an example of a university theologian providing a primary resource for the ordinary Christian disciple needing to live out the life of faith in strained and desperate circumstances.

As if it were not enough that one Principal of Regent's Park College should write with such creative and prophetic passion about the place of suffering within the experience of Christian discipleship, the mantle has been taken by another within the same century. Here, I refer to the editor of this series of study-guides, Paul Fiddes, who has made his own contribution in our generation to a Baptist spirituality of suffering for our own time, in remarkable continuity with the work of his predecessor, Wheeler Robinson.

Re-reading Fiddes' book *The Creative Suffering of God*, originally delivered as a series of Whitley Lectures in the academic year 1979-80, I am impressed at the freshness with which it still speaks from the page, and the clarity with which it continues to address some pivotal theological issues of the early twenty-first century. The core concepts, which I confess that as a young minister in the early 1980s I struggled to understand, now thrill my mind, and the experience to which they testify moves my spirit. At the heart of so much that Fiddes writes has been a powerful motif, one which continues to receive ever richer elucidation as his work unfolds: the idea of Christian discipleship as a deep participation in the Trinitarian life of God. This motif provides the framework within which to grasp (and be grasped by) the full force of its closing paragraph, which provides an inspiring challenge to discover God's most persuasive invitation to the way of faith precisely in the deepest and most destructive context of suffering and death:

> . . . we cannot and must not suppose that death only enters into the being of God in the cross of Jesus or that God only overcomes death there. Wherever trust in God is created, death ceases to be the instrument of hostile non-being. But in the cross of Jesus the encounter of God with death reaches its uttermost pitch, and so his suffering becomes most creative and persuasive. Here God goes furthest in speaking his word of acceptance to us, so that his offer can truly be named a 'new covenant', and through the cross he calls out a new word from us to him. In his humility, this is the conversation of the Spirit that God desires and suffers to create.[19]

We are invited, then, inspired by the suffering and death of Jesus, and by the gracious work of God's Spirit within us, to participate in the creative work of God, who brings us to new life and hope through covenant relationships. The creative lure of Christ's appeal has all the characteristics of that Abelardian bias which I suggested earlier to have a special place in the shaping of Baptist spiritualities.

Today, we can set Paul Fiddes' early study alongside his more recent *Participating in God,* which clarifies and develops the core motif still further. Both these volumes, and other intermediate writings too, testify strongly to a faith which not only explores suffering as a philosophical conundrum occupying the minds of an intellectual élite, but also identifies it as a passionate experience grasping the lives of a praying disciple-community and shaping their very existence. In his later work, this participation in God's life is ever more boldly imaged by the language of dance, a *perichoresis* the eastern church would call it, as the disciple is invited as partner into the dance of God's inner life. Again, it is hard to better the words with which the book receives its final conclusion. The last chapter explores the concept of sacramentality as a powerful way of imagining this extraordinary weave in which God and the believer find themselves wound together in both suffering and hope:

> The sacramental life is one that is open to the presence of God, and can open a door for others into the eternal movements of love and justice that are there ahead of us, and before us, and embracing us. This invitation can be felt like the invitation to a dance, but sometimes like the raw edges of a wound.
>
> This is participation in God. This is theology.[20]

I am back dancing around the tables in an African classroom, singing our way back into hope—though never underestimating the rawness of the pain which has shaped the world of the dancers with whom I share.

5. Conclusion

So how is the evidence shaping up? Once we began to run with the theme of suffering, it was not difficult to find a significant variety of illustrations of my basic argument from the stories of Baptists around the world. It would not be hard to lengthen the role-call. Martin Luther King Jr. certainly comes to mind. This emphasis on attention to the suffering of others, moving towards attention to the suffering of Christ and so to the pain of God does not, of course, belong to the Baptists alone, but I think we have seen that it does have a particular rooting in our story. If it has sometimes, through the centuries, become obscured, it nevertheless remains part of our heritage that I suggest we dare not neglect to rediscover.

But how is this motif faring more generally amongst Baptists in contemporary Britain? This is not easy to answer. The relative equilibrium and pain-free day-to-day life of a typical Baptist congregation in twenty-first-century Britain hardly lends itself to a focus on the heroic or to passionate extremes. My own tentative proposal, however, in the light of my experience of the specific Baptist congregations I visit Sunday by Sunday, and also as we meet in larger set-piece events like Assembly, is that something of the formative inspiration of our roots still survives reasonably well. Where I find it most strongly, perhaps against the odds, is hidden in the underlying patterns which still shape our lives at prayer and our openness to scripture. These, it seems to me, still maintain a continual and exacting scrutiny of the immediacy and authenticity of our individual and corporate discipleship—dimensions which do sustain something quite distinctive in our continuing Baptist identity.

I am in no doubt that we could still benefit enormously from even greater contact with wider global communities, especially those that are not able to shelter themselves from suffering, deprived of the strategies of self-protection only on offer in our ‘first world’ contexts. I remain, however, hopeful that energies still latent in our roots are strong enough to keep drawing us back to the more radical dimensions of our origins, and to generate a relevant spirituality for our time.

Notes

[1] Thomas Merton, *Contemplative Prayer* (London: Darton, Longman and Todd, 1973), p. 82.

[2] B.R. White, *The English Baptists of the Seventeenth Century*. Revised and Expanded Edition (Didcot: The Baptist Historical Society, 1996), p. 25.

[3] White, *English Baptists of the Seventeenth Century*, p. 28.

[4] Edward Barber, *To the Kings Most Excellent Majesty* (1641), cited in White, *The English Baptists of the Seventeenth Century*, p. 28f.

[5] Edward Barber, *A True Discovery of the Ministery of the Gospel* (1645), cited in White, *English Baptists of the Seventeenth Century*, p. 31.

[6] White, *English Baptists of the Seventeenth Century*, p. 44f.

[7] White, *English Baptists of the Seventeenth Century*, p. 57.

[8] Henry Jessey, *The Lords Loud Call to England* (1660), in White, *English Baptists of the Seventeenth Century*, p. 97.

[9] White, *The English Baptists of the Seventeenth,* p. 108.

[10] Abraham Cheare, *Words in Season* (1668), in White, *English Baptists of the Seventeenth Century*, p. 115f.

[11] Raymond Brown, 'Bedfordshire Nonconformist Devotion', *Baptist Quarterly*, 35/7 (1994), pp. 315-21.

[12] Jürgen Moltmann, *The Crucified God*, trans. R.A. Wilson and J. Bowden (London: SCM Press, 1974).

[13] The story is well told on the web-site of the Evangelical Baptist Church of Georgia, www.ebcgeorgia.org/Neue_Dateien/newsstart.html.

[14] Henry Wheeler Robinson, *The Cross in the Old Testament* (London: SCM Press, 1955), pp. 113ff.

[15] See especially the poetry of R S Thomas, and the hymns of Brian Wren, both of whom explore the idea of God's participation in the suffering of the world with great freedom and insight.

[16] Henry Wheeler Robinson, *Suffering Human and Divine* (London: SCM Press, 1940), pp. 181ff.

[17] Robinson, *Suffering Human and Divine*, p. 183.

[18] Robinson, *Suffering Human and Divine,* pp. 218ff.

[19] Paul Fiddes, *The Creative Suffering of God* (Oxford: Oxford University Press, 1988), p. 267.

[20] Paul S. Fiddes, *Participating in God. A Pastoral Doctrine of the Trinity* (London: Darton, Longman and Todd, 2000), p. 302.

4
Spirituality as Discipleship: the Anabaptist Heritage

Nigel Wright

On being presented with the theme of Baptist spirituality one might wonder at the conjunction of the two words, 'Baptist' and 'spirituality'. Although it is hoped that this might change, Baptist spirituality is not an expression that trips off the tongue so easily as, say, 'Ignatian spirituality', or 'Celtic spirituality' or even 'Pentecostal spirituality'. We would do ourselves a great injustice however if we thereby thought that Baptists are not spiritually minded people. Like the man who was surprised to discover that all his life he had been speaking prose, Baptists have their own forms of spirituality or piety even if they are not in the habit of taking them out and dusting them from time to time for their own satisfaction. The fact is that there is a forgetfulness about most Baptists, in the United Kingdom at least, which I personally find endearing rather than worrying: a desire not to overstate the Baptist half of the expression 'Baptist Christian', and so not to identify too readily a specifically Baptist spirituality.

1. Contributing spiritualities

At the same time, we should recognize that in the interwoven complexities of Christian movements Baptists are conscious of their solidarity with broader movements and traditions formative of Baptist spirituality. Their way of giving attention to Christ is adjacent to a number of others. The theme 'under the rule of Christ', which undergirds these essays, points us for instance in the direction of the Reformed tradition for which an ordered life, individual and communal, under the rule of Christ mediated through the word of God by the Spirit of God has been an abiding concern. The bulk of English Baptists emerged for sure out of the wider Reformed tradition associated with Calvin and Geneva, whilst incorporating the more radically reformed ideas of believers' baptism, congregational government and religious liberty into their pool of convictions. Even the emergence of both Particular and General Baptist groupings needs to be seen, along with the Arminian and Calvinist debates about predestination and the extent of the atonement, as a disagreement *within* the broader Reformed tradition, rather than *between* the Reformed and a rival position, as is often suggested by popular usage. Baptist spirituality needs to be aware therefore of its roots in Reformed spirituality.

Then, more immediately recognisable, there is evangelical spirituality.[1] Baptists are evangelicals. Their spirituality contains the twin foci of devotion to scripture as a life-giving authority and personal conversion linked in their case to freely-chosen baptism. They are committed to personal witness and evangelism. They can trace roots both in Puritanism and Pietism, the precursors of modern-day evangelicalism. All the indications are that Baptist churches participate in and contribute to pan-evangelical enterprises on a large scale and large numbers of British Baptists would likely identify themselves as evangelicals before they did so as Baptists. This accounts for the easy flow of membership transfers between Baptist churches and other self-consciously evangelical congregations. Baptist spirituality overlaps with evangelical spirituality and perhaps should be considered a particular and distinctive instance of it. Characteristic evangelical concerns for the practice of the spiritual life, supremely the desire to spend time in Bible reading and personal prayer, have been staple aspects of the life of dedicated Baptists, as much as other evangelicals.

But here we come to my own particular area in this project as a whole: Anabaptist spirituality. This too is a resource on which we may draw for understanding the forms of piety we have espoused and for shaping our spiritual practices for the future. I have long been drawn to Anabaptism. In so far as there has been a renaissance of Anabaptist studies in this country over the last thirty years I can claim to have had a small part in it.[2] This began for me as an aspect of another abiding concern, which has been the renewal of the congregation as the primary form of Christian existence. The Anabaptist movements captured my imagination as examples of free congregations gathered under the rule of Christ and pursuing the life of wholehearted discipleship. Over the years, Anabaptist studies, despite the fact that one would be hard put to find a university department that could supervise a thesis in the subject, have undergone a modest revolution in this country consequent upon a previous such renaissance within the Mennonite communities of North America. It is impossible not to mention at this point the names of Alan and Ellie Kreider whose patient, saintly and scholarly advocacy and embodiment of contemporary Anabaptist convictions have left a permanent mark on British Christianity, and not only on Baptists.[3] Indeed, so complete has been the retrieval of Anabaptist awareness in some circles that the present danger lies not in the neglect of this part of our heritage but in its overstatement. Celtic Christianity and Anabaptism now risk being thought of as the only 'politically correct' Christian movements in the history of the church. The slightly cynical judgement that Celtic Christianity is a construct manufactured somewhere in the South East of England might be applied *mutatis mutandis* to Anabaptism.

American Mennonites passed through a stage of reading their own history which, whatever the undoubted scholarship behind it, also bore traces of high denominational ideology. This was especially manifest in the preference for seeing the so-called 'evangelical Anabaptists' originating in Zürich as the 'Anabaptists proper' quite distinct from the violent 'maccabean Anabaptists' of Münster and other places from whom Mennonites wished to distance themselves. It is true that all historical readings are to some degree ideological, but it is not impossible to pass beyond them to a more chastened and nuanced appreciation of past movements which values them while not overstating their actual achievements. Anabaptism, with all the necessary qualifications, might still figure for us as a source of inspiration and renewal.

It is not my desire to re-enter the debate about the origins of English Baptists and their relationship to continental Anabaptism. Suffice it at this point to re-state the judgement that the Baptists find their primary point of origin in English Puritan Separatism.[4] However, as I have sought to demonstrate elsewhere, Baptist theology can be understood to stand part way between the Reformed and the Anabaptist.[5] Baptists represent a modified form of Reformed theology in that those elements of Calvinist teaching to do with baptism, church government and state are revised in the direction of believers' baptism, congregational government and separation of church and state. These are all movements in a direction upon which Anabaptist ideas may well have had some influence. On the other hand, unlike dominant surviving forms of Anabaptism, Baptists did not reject service as magistrates and were not and have not generally been pacifists, a fact more than amply revealed in the English Civil Wars which followed on closely from the appearance of the English Baptists and in which they played a significant part. However whatever the clear blue water between them, Baptists and Anabaptists manifestly belong to the same family and it is possible to claim Anabaptism as part of our heritage with a high degree of conviction. Anabaptist spirituality can therefore coherently shape and influence our own as part of what we have been given historically.

In the course of my own studies I have been persuaded that theologically I am more of a Baptist than an Anabaptist or a Mennonite, especially when it comes to participation in the social order. However when I reflect about what has drawn me to Anabaptism I can identify certain strengths which resonate for me as a Baptist and which exert a magnetic pull on the ways in which I wish to do theology and, indeed, pursue discipleship. This personal agenda will shape this presentation and since neither spirituality nor theology can be pursued without a distinct element of personal pilgrimage I regard this as fully appropriate. Here I shall concern myself with the centrality of Christ, the primacy of the congregation and the theme of *Nachfolge Christi*, or following after Christ, as a motif for discipleship.

2. The centrality of Christ

The first and foremost of these concerns focuses upon Christ as the centre of our theological thinking, our biblical interpretation and our Christian devotion. If the orthodox Christian claim about the person and work of Christ is true, namely that Christ is the very incarnation of the pre-existent Word of God who was with God in the beginning and is God, then this seems to me absolutely required. Christ is the one in whom God defines God's own self in space and time. 'We have seen his glory as the Father's only Son, full of grace and truth'.[6] The implications of this are, of course, massive, leading to a redefinition of what we mean in the light of Christ by the word *God*, of what God is like and of how methodologically we construct our theology and read our Bibles: we take Christ as the interpretative centre of the unfolding scriptural testimony. Christ is the 'narrow christocentric defile' (to quote Keith Clements expounding Dietrich Bonhoeffer)[7] through which all our theology must pass in order for us to think Christianly about God or indeed about anything. When it comes to reading the Bible, we read it under the rule of Christ.

Now of course, this is an affirmation which can be misapplied in so far and in as much as the Christ through whom we interpret scripture becomes a Christ of our own construction and imagination. So we may play this imagined 'Christ' off against parts of the Bible that we do not like and whose authority we wish to evade by reference to one who is not the incarnation of God but of the ideals and preferences that are currently acceptable and appealing to us. This is a genuine danger as has been abundantly demonstrated by critical scholarship and we acknowledge it. The only Christ to whom we properly have access is the one to whom scripture bears witness. We may construct neither an 'historical' Jesus who is behind and other than the biblical testimony nor an idealized Jesus who is the standard-bearer of whatever causes are currently fashionable. But reading the biblical testimony faithfully leads us to conclude that the trajectory of revelation emerging from the scriptures reaches its zenith and is at its clearest in the 'sun of righteousness' which rises with 'healing in its wings'.[8] All scripture is to be interpreted therefore in the light of the light which shines brightest and every attempt to relegate Christ to some secondary role *subordinate* to scripture rather than *supreme* within scripture needs to be resisted.

It does seem to me that in this apparently subtle distinction there are enormous implications and potential divergences. Indeed, which way we turn at this junction determines what form of evangelicalism we end up with. Karl Barth was entirely right to challenge and modify Reformed theology at this point. It is possible to be biblical without being Christian. The Christian faith represents a development within Judaism which embraced the revelation of God contained in the Hebrew scriptures while radically modifying it in the light of a Messiah who suffered and died and rose again for our salvation. The primary form of the Word of God, according to Barth, is the incarnate Word to which the secondary form of the Word, scripture, bears witness. In this construct we read the scriptures not for themselves but for their testimony to the Word which is their centre. Contrast this with that understanding of the authority of scripture which sees all parts of scripture as possessing equal authority. The argument asserts that Christ validated the Hebrew scriptures by accepting them as the authority by which he lived, and further validated the Greek scriptures by telling his apostles that the Spirit would lead them into all truth, so each part of scripture is to be received with the same reverence. Christ therefore becomes one extended instance within a series of instances of revelation all of which possess equal authority. On this basis theology and preaching can be conducted in some of their aspects without significant reference to Christ, and often are. Granted that texts do need to be interpreted in their own terms, in the wider task of theology and preaching it is only as their content is brought into relationship with Christ that they become Christian.

To take one example, what the Bible teaches about predestination can be gathered from a series of texts without substantial reference to Christ himself. Christ then becomes part of a predestinarian scheme which claims to be grounded in the Word of God but is in fact under-informed by Christ himself. In an alternative, Barthian understanding, nothing can be understood about God except it be first of all informed by that of God which is made known in the primary form of the Word. When this is done, I would suggest, understandings about an eternal decree made before the foundation of the world to consign a proportion of humankind to eternal damnation become unsustainable, however neatly logical they can be made to seem. As Barth argued, what is first of all revealed in Christ is that God is for us.[9]

To take a second example, the doctrine of God is routinely pursued in the textbooks by first constructing a definition of God in which God is portrayed as infinite, omniscient, omnipotent, omnipresent. Christ is then to be accounted for within the terms of a God we have already defined apart from him; and the primary datum about God, which is that God is both triune and free, is left as a conundrum to be accounted for. By contrast if we begin with the God who is to be encountered in and through the one who is the Word of God in the belief that here God is to be defined, we begin not with a series of abstractions but with a living experience of

God's being with us, and so with the question, 'who must this God be who can meet us in human form, sharing our life and embracing our death for our own salvation and that of the world?'

When we speak of being under the rule of Christ, we must first mean by this the rule of Christ *within the scriptures and their interpretation,* not the rule of the scriptures over Christ. We should be grateful in this that the Baptist Union Declaration of Principle, followed by a number of other unions, declare the basis of our Union to include the belief that 'our God and Saviour, Jesus Christ, God manifest in the flesh, is the sole and absolute authority in all matters pertaining to faith and practice, as revealed in the Holy Scriptures'. The phrasing is both significant and salutary, safeguarding both the centrality of the incarnate (and now ascended) Word as our supreme authority and also the irreplaceable role of the scriptures in bearing decisive witness to that revelation. This surely has significance in describing Baptist spirituality as both radically Christ-centred and radically biblically-orientated but with Christ as the Lord of scripture and the Lord within scripture.

In this section then, I have applied the term 'under the rule of Christ', first of all to the scriptures as a way of approaching their interpretation and application. I contend that this was a significant contribution of the Anabaptist way[10] and that it resonates with the theological revolution in the Reformed tradition that we associate with Karl Barth. In some approaches to the Anglican liturgy, the reading of the Gospel is treated differently from other Bible readings. The Gospels are carried into the midst of the congregation. The people stand and turn towards the reader while the Gospel is being read as a sign that they are giving particular attention to these parts of the biblical text. Perhaps in our ostensibly non-liturgical tradition there is something we might learn from this.

3. The primacy of the congregation

A second feature that attracted me to Anabaptism was its concern for the congregation of committed and faithful disciples and to a communal existence within a rule and order of life expressed through those congregations. The rejection of priestly hierarchy did not denote for them a desire to live anarchically but within communities in which power was commonly owned and order was primarily understood as devotion to a godly and holy life within a supportive discipline. As a minister, realizing the potential of the congregation has, of course, always been a motivating factor. The possibility that a group of people might exist within the wider community as a spiritually vibrant, mutually supportive, theologically instructed and ethically distinctive presence, now gathered for worship, now scattered in service and witness, has always had immense appeal. If Luke in Acts 2: 41-47 intended to set before us an ideal of congregational life then he certainly succeeded:

> So those who welcomed (Peter's) message were baptized and that day about three thousand persons were added. They devoted themselves to the apostles' teaching and fellowship, to the breaking of bread and the prayers. Awe came upon everyone, because many wonders and signs were being done by the apostles. All who believed were together and had all things in common; they would sell their possessions and goods and distribute the proceeds to all, as any had need. Day by day, as they spent much time together in the temple, they broke bread at home and ate their food with glad and generous hearts, praising God and having the goodwill of all the people. And day by day the Lord added to their number those who were being saved.

In his excellent description of Anabaptist spirituality, Arnold Snyder develops the idea that Anabaptism grew in part out of the monastic concern to live the holy life within community, only in the Anabaptist experiment the communities were to be set within the context of daily life and work, of family and community. This is a form of laicized monasticism. Baptism for the Anabaptist was equivalent to the monastic vow giving entry as it did to a professed community under the discipline of the observed life.[11]

Within such communities the primary preoccupation was the imitation of Christ, as it had been in late medieval monasticism. It provided a significant spiritual impulse for the Anabaptists, many of them formerly members of religious orders. Living, therefore, under the rule of Christ within specific and identifiable communities was a crucial aspect of being in Christ's way of discipleship. The theme 'under the rule of Christ' carries echoes of the monastic tradition which shared the Anabaptist concern for intense closeness to Jesus. Piety was not to be pursued or expressed in individualism or isolation but communally, so that communion, foot-washing, singing and corporate prayer should be seen as indispensable aspects of Anabaptist spirituality. (It is to be noted that in the use of hymns and songs, Anabaptists were well ahead of their Baptist cousins being, from the beginning, a song-writing and hymn-singing community.)

Shedding ourselves of romantic notions, we know from history that the community life of Anabaptists was sometimes the occasion for what we would regard as abusive practice. We may have no desire to go where some of them went in the practice of the 'ban', or 'shunning' or in engendering legalistic social conformity, or even in the common ownership of goods characteristic of the Hutterites. At the same time, there are immense challenges here in framing a Baptist spirituality. If we are to acknowledge the rule of Christ as revealed in the scriptures, we also acknowledge him as his presence is experienced and discerned in the congregations which gather around him and the word which bears testimony to him. It is no accident that the Declaration of Principle, already quoted in part, goes on to say that 'each Church has liberty, under the guidance of the Holy Spirit to interpret and administer His Laws.' Here we are surely to understand the 'laws' of Christ to mean not simply or only the teaching of Jesus as given in the New Testament but the laws, or guidance, he continues to give through the Holy Spirit to the congregations which submit to his rule. Within a Baptist spirituality, living as 'acoustic' communities which exist by hearing the Word of God and also being 'hermeneutical communities'[12] which bear the responsibility of interpreting and administering that Word, count as primary ways in which we attend to the presence and work of Christ in the world.

The Christian life is surely then to be understood as congregational life, as consisting in membership of a living community which gathers under the rule of Christ to worship him and to seek his will. In such congregations Christ continues to be particularly present in the world he has redeemed. Congregations are to be understood as far more than convenience stores into which we may drop for necessary supplies while our lives are focused elsewhere. There is an element of mutual indwelling, of finding ourselves by participation in churches which gather with the promise that Christ is particularly *there*, in the midst of them. The word 'spirituality' can often connote for us something that we do with our solitariness, an individualistic seeking after God perhaps on retreat or in a quiet place, and no-one can deny the place that such spiritual exercises have in our lives. But in a congregationalist tradition it must also embrace the notion of membership, of participating in the body and of being joined by the Spirit in the bond of peace to a company in which there is an expression of divine *order*.

4. Following after Christ

A third dimension of Anabaptism which attracted me was its stress on discipleship as *Nachfolge Christi*, following after Christ, a phrase which picks up the invitation of the Lord himself.[13] It has often been observed that evangelicalism has had a preference in reading the scriptures for the epistles, especially the writings of Paul. This was where *doctrine,* the real meat of the word was to be found. By contrast the Gospels were *stories*, and so manifestly inferior. Such literary prejudice has been accompanied by a theological prejudice which has understood Christ through his death and resurrection as the ground of our justification and salvation while neglecting the call to imitate his life and to follow his manner and pattern of sacrificial self-giving. It is sometimes pointed out that in the Apostles' Creed the whole life of Jesus is contracted to a comma between 'born of the Virgin Mary' and 'suffered under Pontius Pilate'. Without neglecting the dimensions of Christ's death which mark it as an atoning sacrifice, the Anabaptists understood the cross of Christ also to be a pattern of the whole shape of Jesus' redemptive life, and therefore of the life of the believers who earnestly follow him. This is a life of self-giving and self-denial, of returning good in place of evil, of absorbing and enduring hostility rather than returning it.

Arnold Snyder points out how in the late medieval period there was a large emphasis on the humanity and suffering of Christ of which Thomas à Kempis' work *Of the Imitation of Christ* was simply the best known example. He finds the parallels with this emphasis in Anabaptism striking.[14] The Anabaptists coined the term *Gelassenheit*, or 'yielded abandonment' to express the appropriate relationship of the believer to

Christ. At the heart of Anabaptism is a process of 'learning to will what God wills', which is similar to the emphasis of the monastic tradition.[15] In this sense it has been claimed by Walter Klaassen that Anabaptism is 'neither Catholic nor Protestant' in that it neither imagines that justification is the end product of a process of sanctification nor that faith alone without inner transformation is an adequate understanding of the divine remedy for sin.[16] Snyder points out that this could equally be understood as 'both Catholic and Protestant' in the Anabaptist intention deliberately to combine ascetic Catholic piety with reforming Protestant ideas.[17] We can, I think, closely identify the idea of living under the rule of Christ with that of *Gelassenheit* and identify this as the posture which believers may assume in their participation both in the life of the living God and in the community which finds its centre and soul in God's being.

5. Formative values and convictions

Having identified the centrality of Christ, the primacy of the congregation and the motif of following after Christ, and related these to the theme of the rule of Christ, an appropriate summary of these and other elements can be found in the Anabaptist Network's statement of values and convictions. These deserve to be well known and appreciated in Baptist congregations.

- Jesus is our example, teacher, friend, redeemer and Lord. He is the source of our life, the central reference point for our faith and lifestyle, for our understanding of church and our engagement with society. We are committed to following Jesus as well as worshipping him.
- Jesus is the focal point of God's revelation. We are committed to a Jesus-centred approach to the Bible, and to the community of faith as the primary context in which we read the Bible and discern and apply its implications for discipleship.
- Western culture is slowly emerging from the Christendom era when church and state jointly presided over a society in which almost all were assumed to be Christian. Whatever its positive contributions on values and institutions, Christendom seriously distorted the gospel, marginalized Jesus, and has left the churches ill-equipped for mission in a

post-Christendom culture. As we reflect on this, we are committed to learning from the experience and perspectives of movements such as Anabaptism that rejected standard Christendom assumptions and pursued alternative ways of thinking and behaving.
- The frequent association of the church with status, wealth and force is inappropriate for followers of Jesus and damages our witness. We are committed to exploring ways of being good news to the poor, powerless and persecuted, aware that such discipleship may attract opposition, resulting in suffering and sometimes ultimately martyrdom.
- Churches are called to be committed communities of discipleship and mission, places of friendship, mutual accountability and multi-voiced worship. As we eat together, sharing bread and wine, we sustain hope as we seek God's kingdom together. We are committed to nurturing and developing such churches, in which young and old are valued, leadership is consultative, roles are related to gifts rather than gender and baptism is for believers.
- Spirituality and economics are inter-connected. In an individualist and consumerist culture and in a world where economic injustice is rife, we are committed to finding ways of living simply, sharing generously, caring for creation, and working for justice.
- Peace is at the heart of the gospel. As followers of Jesus in a divided and violent world, we are committed to finding non-violent alternatives and to learning how to make peace between individuals, within and among churches, in society, and between nations, and with the natural world.[18]

6. Challenges for a Baptist spirituality

Having outlined these themes let me now draw out, perhaps more provocatively and more programmatically than in what has preceded, some areas which might challenge us as we re-imagine some of their implications for understanding and shaping Baptist spirituality.

Firstly, there are words here with which we do not sit as easily as previous generations have done. In this language and in the Reformed, evangelical and Anabaptist spiritualities to which I have referred, we find quite crucially the recognition of *authority*. We are 'under' the 'rule' of Christ. In an age which values perhaps more than anything else both personal autonomy and self-actualization, and which reads the language of lordship as domination and oppression, the concept of heteronomy—that I am called to find myself through submission to the rule of another—is both alien and offensive. Similarly *Gelassenheit*, yieldedness, and the notion of an obedient following of another is construed by many as a diminishing of self-worth and dignity.

Now there are two ways in which we might sympathize with this modern instinct. It is clear to us that the Father of our Lord Jesus Christ calls us to a willing submission, an act of freedom in which we choose to acknowledge the authority of the one whom we call Lord. Within the historical experience of Baptists there has been a struggle in society between one principle which argues, 'faith is so important that all must share the same one' and that which argues, 'faith is so important that all must be free to embrace that which seems most persuasive to them'. Baptists set their faces against any notion of compulsory religion in the belief that only that which is freely given is spiritually valuable. In similar vein, while consistently respectful towards the authorities, Baptists have firmly espoused the doctrine of 'the crown rights of the Redeemer' causing them to be jealous of Christ's claim to their ultimate loyalty and affection. Neither in matters spiritual nor temporal have they wished to acknowledge the lordship of any other than Christ, who alone is worthy and to whom alone such devotion is properly given. In this sense Baptist acknowledgement of the Lordship of Christ follows a 'disjunctive' rather than a 'conjunctive' logic, that is to say rather than validating the claims of powerful earthly rulers it subverts and relativizes them.[19] These qualifications aside, there is a demand which God-in-Christ makes upon us which can only be expressed by use of the language of authority, obedience, submission and duty. Any spirituality which does not contain these elements is deceiving itself, since we all acknowledge something which is ultimate even if it is ourselves. Learning to live under authority, the authority of Christ over individuals and congregations mediated by the Spirit through the scriptures is a fundamental configuring of any form of Christian, let alone Baptist, spirituality. Furthermore, since it is in scripture that we find the normative witness to the Lord whose authority we gladly embrace, any Baptist spirituality is bound to be deeply scriptural. There is no Christ other than he to whom the scriptures point. Despite the difficulties within it with which we wrestle, the biblical text is a place of sacramental encounter as we find the Lord speaking to us from within it.

Secondly, the primacy of the congregation and its indispensable role in any form of Baptist spirituality leads us to think carefully about the life of our churches. The plain fact is that few congregations are able to bear the weight that our theology places upon them. The levels of spiritual passion, biblical and theological literacy, ethical discernment and formation in the Christ-like virtues are, in many of our congregations, much lower than our theology suggests they ought to be. Neither does it particularly help congregations to have expectations which are beyond the capacity of erring, sinning humans to deliver. The corrosive acids at work undermining congregational life are considerable. Some of these derive from the external effects of contemporary culture upon congregational life;[20] others are corrosive from within as congregations lose confidence or exist for themselves rather than dynamically under the rule of Christ. Indeed, a current threat to the churches exists in the tendency towards a post-congregationalism which has given up on the congregational experiment, at least in its inherited form, precisely because the sluggish realities of church life prove at worst a hindrance to spiritual growth and at best a boring irrelevance.[21]

In a time when the rhetoric of what we should be doing often surrounds church-planting on the one hand and emerging church thinking on the other (both of which remain congregational in orientation), the fact remains that the majority of our churches consist of established congregations which stand in need of renewal in all manner of ways, theological, spiritual, organizational and ethical. Enabling such congregational renewal is a massive challenge for ministers and one which is currently under-addressed in Baptist circles. Unless we can achieve spiritual communities which are well-ordered and attractive embodiments of Christian devotion and mission there is little else we can achieve. Yet there is much to suggest that the congregation, with all its possibilities, distinctives and durability, has a great deal still to offer, whatever the corrosive forces ranged against it. Baptists need to give more direct attention to fostering the health of congregations and to that relatively new discipline known as 'congregational studies'.[22]

Within this, the issue of how we understand and practise church membership is crucial for a spirituality that values the communal. In face of the current reluctance to embrace the demands of church membership ought we to lessen the demands we make upon people or defy contemporary trends by increasing them? What we have seen in Anabaptism might encourage us to upgrade our understanding of what is involved in being a church member even if this means that the number of 'members' will be considerably fewer than the number of worshippers in our churches. In addition to the cultural presumption that seeks to avoid committed forms of institutional belonging there surfaces from time to time in our churches a resistance to the concept of membership on the grounds that it is not 'biblical'. This claim needs to be both conceded and resisted. Church membership as practised by Baptist congregations in the West clearly reflects the nature of organizations and societies in post-industrial societies. In this sense it is hard to claim it is 'biblical'. On the other hand, Christian discipleship entails devoting oneself to the Christian community and living out one's life as part of it, and this is thoroughly biblical in concept and expectation.[23] Formal patterns of church membership are simply more or less useful ways of achieving this end. Furthermore, the notion of covenant commitment is deeply rooted in Baptist church life and overwhelms the tendency to see membership in the more bureaucratic terms of 'having one's name on the roll'. Baptists need to decide whether membership is something worth preserving, and if so how to do so.

In another place I have argued that as a matter of fact, people belong to congregations in different ways and that these forms of belonging need to be recognized.[24] This might mean, for instance, celebrating and making more of 'community membership' whilst simultaneously strengthening 'covenant membership'. This suggestion follows the well-established tendency to distinguish between 'members' and 'adherents', although it adds a little more dignity to the latter. It enables churches to affirm the broader forms of belonging to a church community, which themselves are formative and in many cases essential preparation for embracing commitment, whilst setting before people the more demanding challenge of covenant membership, which some might call 'stakeholder' membership, as an appropriate further step of commitment. Allied with proper forms of education and formation this might at least ensure that at the core of our congregations are those who take seriously both the concept and the practice of living under the rule of Christ. Perhaps in the midst of discussions about 'emergent church' we ought now to begin to talk about 're-emergent church', that is to say a re-appropriation of classical themes of church as ordered and disciplined community with a strong emphasis on the place of the sacraments, preaching, membership and the ministry.[25] This need not be seen as a challenge to the concept of emergent churches, but it would be a stimulus to ensure that new expressions of church do not depart from a commitment both to the congregation as an essential expression of Christian life and to an 'ecclesial minimum' without which such expressions would not be 'church'.[26] Neither should a return to the classical be seen as shirking the challenge of change but rather as embracing that challenge as classical Christian themes are re-appropriated in new forms. For instance, to celebrate the ministry of preaching need not mean that we continue with the old patterns of monologue and 'pulpiteering' but find the ways in which preaching can be made vital and dynamic for today's context.

In this discussion however there remains an elephant in the room. The subject of church discipline and the problems associated with it are considerable and yet unavoidable if we are to take seriously the notion of being 'under the rule of Christ' with all its implications for a way of life that is intentional, serious and disciplined. It is beyond doubt that our Baptist forbears regarded church membership as a covenant in which they agreed to walk together according to a common rule of morality and life. The traditional language of 'watching over one another in love' held good both for what we today would regard as pastoral care and support and for guarding one another from moral lapse. Departures from what was perceived to be godly were for the church to discuss and to act upon in and through the church meeting. All sanctions that involved force or compulsion were of course renounced, but the sanctions of disapproval, rebuke and, as a last resort, excommunication were retained. It was understood and accepted that this discipline was part of belonging to a congregation. Now it is a topic we prefer to skirt around.

The reasons for such reticence are not hard to fathom. Who wants to be thought to interfere in the lives of others? For that matter, in our anonymous and mobile society, who really knows what is going on in the lives of others, especially those whom we might only see irregularly? Older patterns of church discipline depended on being part of relatively small congregations where the members would both know and observe each other's lives on a continuing basis. This is not well adapted to contemporary life in church or society. Experience suggests that even where there are close pastoral relationships or structures of accountability there can also be secretive patterns of behaviour. How then might church discipline be reconceived in a world where the 'observed life' is a rarity?

An immediate suggestion is to recast discipline within the broader framework of discipleship. The church is a community of disciples, of those who have declared their intention through baptism of living as disciples of Christ. Churches are Christian communities which first gather disciples and then offer the support and resources to endure in this discipleship throughout one's life. Church members are those who have declared their allegiance to a particular congregation to accept it as their own community of reference and to support its missionary objectives. If it is the case that such a community is open at the edges and ready to welcome many as 'community members', it nonetheless needs to take care in preparing people for 'covenant membership' since these are they on whom the persistence of the church depends. At this point more instruction needs to be given about what it means to be in covenant with each other and that to do this entails embracing intentionally a rule of life. Church membership is not something that should be entered into passively but with high levels of understanding about what it means and what it requires, including the fact that while rejecting any right to control, it does bestow upon the community the right to advise, warn and in extreme cases exclude. If this in turn means that fewer people embrace its demands this need not be of undue concern since quality must sometimes outrank quantity, although in an ideal world one would hope not to have to choose between the two. However, may it not be the case that precisely because it is seen as a rigorous calling, committed church membership acquires a different kind of attractiveness, one which will cut across the grain of our supposedly uncommitted culture?

The third challenge for Baptist spirituality to be derived from Anabaptism concerns how we might envisage what it might mean to follow after Christ. Certainly, when seeking a moral vision from the scriptures, we need to avoid the all too common tendency to search the scriptures for guidance without reference to their interpretative centre in Christ. It is by no means that the scriptures as a whole have nothing to say to us, but rather that even what the scriptures have to say must pass through the 'narrow defile' which is Jesus Christ in order to be fully grasped. Yet we also err if we take following after Jesus to mean literal adherence to a series of rules or laws handed to us by him. Even here there is a hermeneutical process which is not always easy to negotiate. Many people remind themselves of the demands of Christ by wearing the bracelet with 'WWJD' on it: What Would Jesus Do? It is not a bad question to ask, but answering it requires imagination as well as obedience. Even Jesus lived within a context. How do we extract from his way of living that which endures for us in contexts widely different from his own?

We can begin to answer this by remembering that the New Testament itself refers us, in imitating Christ, not to the incidentals of his time and place but to the whole trajectory of his life and death expressed in taking the form of a servant and becoming obedient unto death.[27] It is the shape of Christ's life which is our primary datum for discipleship and this might take us beyond a merely legal interpretation. When in the Sermon on the Mount Jesus tells his disciples not to resist evildoers but to turn the other cheek, to give away the cloak and to walk the extra mile,[28] are these universal laws for all situations, the possible embracing of a permanent victimhood? Or are they not rather, as Walter Wink suggests, specific, creative and indeed humorous examples of a 'third way' beyond retaliation and subjection to oppression, a way which refuses to mirror the evil which is done?[29] If this is the case then those who live in the spirit of Jesus are doing far more than juridically applying universal rules to situations where they do not fit. Rather they are practising a form of spirituality. Out of lives formed by an intimate knowledge of the way of Jesus and its application in the context of his own life, they are living in the Spirit of Christ now and trusting for those creative and imaginative ways of finding the third way beyond the recycling of evil and the acceptance of de-humanizing victimhood. I particularly like Wink's contemporary example of how such inspiration and wit might work:

> Bishop Desmond Tutu was walking by a construction site on a temporary sidewalk the width of one person. A white man appeared at the other end, recognized Tutu, and said, 'I don't give way to gorillas.' At which Tutu stepped aside, made a deep sweeping gesture, and said, 'Ah yes, but I do.'[30]

Such inspirations do not emerge out of a legalistic approach to the teaching of Jesus which can be legislated into every conceivable context, but only out of a spirituality or a formation which understands the shape and intention of Jesus' life and which is vitally open to following after him on the trajectory he pursued on his way to the cross. The inspiration of the Spirit is essential to such a lifestyle. Towards such a Christ-centred and Spirit-inspired spirituality we press on.

7. Core values

If the latter section of this chapter has concerned itself with programmatic suggestions of how Baptist spirituality might be stimulated by its interaction with Anabaptism, this final part offers a specific and modest proposal that could have an immediate impact upon Baptist spirituality and ethos.

Some years ago the Baptist Union published a document entitled *5 Core Values for a Gospel People*. The values identified Baptist Christians as sharing in a prophetic, an inclusive, a sacrificial, a missionary and a worshipping community. The document has been widely studied in churches and regularly praised by other denominations. There can be no doubt as to its formative value. Each of the values represents a legitimate and wholesome aspiration, although in another place I have raised the question, following the Archbishop of Canterbury, as to whether it is possible for a confessional and morally committed movement to define itself as 'inclusive' in unambiguous terms.[31] Given that at some point a Christian church must exclude beliefs and behaviours it considers at variance with its basic commitments, it might be more accurate and more honest to substitute the word 'welcoming' for 'inclusive'. This aside, there is another concern.

The concern is that when certain values are placed in the foreground other values and beliefs are assumed in the background. Over time the values that are stated tend to become detached from the other values and beliefs on which they are in fact dependent. It is of interest to note how *5 Core Values* has tended to become '*the* 5 Core Values' of the Baptist Union. The original title avoided the assumption that the five were the sum total of values. When the number five becomes fixed the danger is that the ethos and spirituality they inform becomes lopsided. In this chapter I wish to propose that the document *5 Core Values* be now revisited and revised as a constructive denominational exercise and into this discussion I wish to place two further values for consideration: *faithfulness* and *freedom*.

Christian people are called to be *faithful*, to hold fast to Jesus Christ and the truth as it is in him. This entails both biblical and doctrinal fidelity to the apostolic testimony as contained first of all in the scriptures, then in the Great Tradition of the catholic faith,[32] and then in that variant of the catholic Christian faith which is the Baptist movement. Being under the rule of Christ involves living in continuity with that of God which is made known in Jesus Christ and such continuity is one of belief and practice. This value needs to be stated and not simply assumed since all the other values that are espoused have their fountainhead here. Moreover, there are worrying signs that Baptists as a whole are no longer reading their Bibles seriously and are losing the ability to discuss their faith doctrinally as distinct from experientially. By contrast with former generations, the present generation of Baptists compares unfavourably in terms of both biblical and theological literacy and for the sake of our spiritual health this needs to be reversed.

Christian people are called into *freedom*. The freedom is granted in Jesus Christ. 'For freedom Christ has set us free'.[33] Baptist origins are to be found in the movement towards a church freed from the sacred and ecclesiastical power of the establishment and in the impetus towards a society freed from monarchical tyranny. But this freedom is freedom under the rule of Christ, not the pretended freedoms of moral licence or political anarchism. Whatever may previously have been said in this chapter about the church as an ordered community or the practice of church discipline, this must all be read as a means towards maximizing the freedom in Christ of the community of disciples, not to its diminution.

Revisiting and recasting the core values of the Baptist Union of Great Britain is opportune. Such a step would give impetus to the continuing and much needed renewal of this communion of churches. It would assist us in truly becoming a free people under the rule of a gracious Lord and could shape our spirituality for the journey which lies before us.

Notes

[1] James M. Gordon, *Evangelical Spirituality: From the Wesleys to John Stott* (London: SPCK, 1991).

[2] See J. F. V. Nicholson, *Our Heritage: The Baptists of Yorkshire, Lancashire and Cheshire 1647-1987* (Leeds: Yorkshire Baptist Association and Lancashire and Cheshire Baptist Association, 1987), p. 150.

[3] Alan Kreider and Stuart Murray (eds), *Coming Home: Stories of Anabaptists in Britain and Ireland* (Kitchener: Pandora Press, 2000).

[4] Kenneth R. Manley covers the ground effectively in 'Origins of the Baptists: The Case for Development from Puritanism-Separatism' in William H. Brackney (ed.), *Faith, Life and Witness: The Papers of the Study and Research Division of the Baptist World Alliance 1986-1990* (Birmingham, AL: Samford University Press, 1990), pp. 56-69.

[5] Nigel G. Wright, *Disavowing Constantine: Mission, Church and the Social Order in the Theologies of John Howard Yoder and Jürgen Moltmann* (Carlisle: Paternoster Press, 2000), pp. 42-4.

[6] John 1:14 (NRSV margin).

[7] Keith W. Clements, *A Patriotism for Today: Love of Country in Dialogue with the Witness of Dietrich Bonhoeffer* (London: Collins, 1984 and 1986), p. 57.

[8] Malachi 4:2.

[9] In relation to Barth's theological predecessors P. K. Jewett comments, 'The nature of their mistake, [Barth] believed, was that they divorced God from Jesus Christ—that is to say, when they thought of God's election, they thought abstractly of the eternal decree of the hidden God rather than concretely of the gracious purpose of God revealed in Jesus Christ. As a result, they missed the decisive insight into the heart of the matter, which has to do with the question of the object of predestination.' Jewett, *Election and Predestination* (Grand Rapids: Eerdmans/ Exeter: Paternoster, 1985), p. 19.

[10] See further on this Stuart Murray, *Biblical Interpretation in the Anabaptist Tradition* (Kitchener: Pandora Press, 2000), pp. 70-96.

[11] Arnold Snyder, *Following in the Footsteps of Christ: The Anabaptist Tradition* (London: Darton, Longman and Todd, 2004), p. 82.

[12] Lesslie Newbigin, *The Gospel in a Pluralist Society* (London: SPCK, 1989), pp. 222-3.

[13] Matthew 16: 24-8.

[14] Snyder, *Following in the Footsteps of Christ*, p. 44.

[15] Snyder, *Following in the Footsteps of Christ*, p. 40.

[16] Walter Klaassen, *Anabaptism: Neither Catholic nor Protestant* (Kitchener: Pandora Press, 2001).

[17] Snyder, *Following in the Footsteps of Christ*, pp. 27-8.

[18] The Anabaptist Network publicity leaflet and www.anabaptistnetwork.com.

[19] Matthew 23: 8-10.

[20] Haddon Willmer, 'The Collapse of Congregations', *Anvil*, 18/4 (2001), pp. 249-60.

[21] Alan Jamieson, *A Churchless Faith: Faith Journeys Beyond the Churches* (London: SPCK, 2002).

[22] Matthew Guest, Karin Tusting and Linda Woodhead (eds), *Congregational Studies in the UK: Christianity in a Post-Christian Context* (Aldershot: Ashgate, 2004).

[23] Acts 2: 42.

[24] Nigel G. Wright, *New Baptists, New Agenda* (Carlisle: Paternoster, 2002), chapter 5.

[25] I am grateful to Dr Roger Standing for the term and idea of the 're-emergent church'.

[26] For the concept of the ecclesial minimum see Miroslav Volf, *After Our Likeness: The Church as the Image of the Trinity* (Grand Rapids: Eerdmans, 1998), pp.127-58. It might be recognized that the emerging or 'emergent' church movement is a diverse phenomenon parts of which can be marked by severely critical attitudes towards traditional and contemporary expressions of the church as it has been inherited: John Drane, 'The Emerging Church',

International Journal for the Study of the Christian Church, 6/1 (2006), pp. 3-11.

[27] Philippians 2: 1-11; I Peter 2: 18-25.

[28] Matthew 5: 38-42.

[29] Walter Wink, *Engaging the Powers: Discernment and Resistance in a World of Domination* (Minneapolis: Fortress Press, 1992), pp. 175-93.

[30] Wink, *Engaging the Powers*, p. 191.

[31] 'Inclusively exclusive', *Talk Magazine*, Spring 2007.

[32] Roger E. Olson, *The Mosaic of Christian Belief: Twenty Centuries of Unity and Diversity* (Leicester: Apollos, 2002), p. 14. Olson also calls this the 'strong central core of identifiable Christian belief', p. 31.

[33] Galatians 5: 1.

5
Spirituality and Scripture: the Rule of the Word

James Gordon

With Baptist brothers and sisters across the world:

We believe

- That the Bible is a trustworthy and final authority for faith and practice when interpreted responsibly under the guidance of God's Holy Spirit within the community of faith.[1]

According to this statement several convictions shape Baptist ecclesiology and significantly influence Baptist approaches to spirituality. But does such an affirmation mean that for Baptists, the Bible is the equivalent of a rule of life? A straightforward 'yes' fails to take into account important qualifications and balances within Baptist theological convictions. These include the lordship of Jesus Christ as revealed in scripture and exercised within his church through word and Spirit, the community of faith which follows after Christ as the preferred hermeneutic context, and the active ministry of the Holy Spirit in illuminating scripture for individual and community. These convictions define more sharply the role of scripture in its relation to Christ and church, as the Bible is read, studied, preached, heard and assimilated into the life and witness of Baptist communities seeking to live under the rule of the Word.

The first three sections of this chapter seek to bring Christ and scripture into a relationship that allows each to exert proper authority in the life of the individual believer and the community of faith. The remainder of the chapter introduces several Baptists who have used and practised scripture in their discipleship and devotion. John Gill, Anne Steele, C. H. Spurgeon and George Beasley-Murray illustrate how very different Baptists have actually used scripture. What it means to live under the rule of the Word is explored through reflecting on the different ways each used scripture in learning and loving Christ.

1. A Baptist theology of the Word

Historically the radical appeal to 'scripture alone' (*sola scriptura*) as the normative source of Baptist ecclesiology, spiritual practice and doctrinal reflection, exerted its own pressure towards sharper doctrinal definition. To safeguard a number of principles—the primacy of scripture, evangelical truth experienced as personal faith in Christ, and the way that these are expressed within the community of Christ—Baptists created and affirmed their own confessions of faith. For Baptists these documents were statements that defined who they were, defending and declaring their way of practising their faith. Baptist confessions were framed within a determined loyalty to scripture,[2] and the resulting self-portrait was given colour, tone and perspective by evangelical experience. The lived reality of such confessions was expressed in models of church developed along lines Baptists believed could be clearly discerned in the experience of the New Testament churches.

For Baptists there is an important tension between several strong convictions: (a) faith is personal trust in Christ who is himself the sole and absolute authority; (b) scripture is the uniquely authoritative witness to Christ; (c) confessions, though provisional human documents, nevertheless state the truth of who Baptists are, and carry an authority derived intentionally from scripture. Amongst Baptists, evangelical spiritual experience has been a powerful undercurrent pulling them towards doctrinal definition and a biblically-driven orthodoxy. This evangelical undertow continues to shape Baptist spiritualities as intrinsically Christ-centred while also being instinctively Bible-centred.

According to one recent popular handbook on Baptist faith and practice, *Radical Believers*, 'In order to discern and interpret the authority of Christ among them, Baptists appeal in the first place to the Scriptures, believing these to be the means by which all sources of truth about God are to be assessed and judged'.[3] However, there is an underlying and inevitable tension between the Baptist conviction about the finality and sufficiency of Christ *as revealed in* scripture, and a self-consciously evangelical position in which the Bible itself is predicated with sole, final and sufficient authority.

As the primary written authority for knowing God's revelation in Christ, scripture certainly exerts decisive control over the minds of Christians seeking to live in a Baptist way. *Sola scriptura* as a spiritual slogan expresses in shorthand the resistance of the Christian mind and heart to having the deepest knowledge and personal experience of Christ reduced from the rich diversity of scriptural truth to an imposed uniformity, defined through negotiated agreements and forms of words given confessional status. Early Baptists concurred with the exhortation: 'Labour to know your Christian liberty . . . where God hath left latitude let us take notice of it.'[4]

When Baptists live under the rule of the Word as both Christ and scripture, they seek to follow Christ in liberty and loyalty. The study and appropriation of scripture then becomes a discipleship of the intellect. Through prayer, reflection, preaching, and private reading of scripture, they nurture a personally responsive faith-relationship of love and trust in Christ. They live out that faith in the supportive fellowship and corrective discipline of a local community of believers covenanting together in following Christ through interpreted scripture. And at their best, they do so with 'that latitude of expression which the Scriptures indulge and recommend'.[5]

Legitimate 'latitude of expression' in personal faith and the conviction that the local church is competent as a true church of Christ, are given formal expression in the Declaration of Principle of the Baptist Union of Great Britain, which affirms the controlling convictions which shape Baptist life together. The first of three clauses reads:

> That our Lord and Saviour Jesus Christ, God manifest in the flesh, is the sole and absolute authority in all matters pertaining to faith and practice as revealed in the Holy Scriptures and that each Church has liberty, under the guidance of the Holy Spirit, to interpret and administer His laws.[6]

The Declaration is careful to relate the authority and sufficiency of scripture to the finality and sufficiency of Christ, creating a mutually affirming dialectic. The deliberate affirmation of a high Christology commits Baptists to the practice of a radical ecclesiology rooted in the experience of the believing community seeking the mind of the living Christ, under the rule of the Word. This affirmation establishes a specific kind of relationship between Christ and scripture, within which scripture points beyond and above itself to Christ and his way, but where scripture is given the privileged and decisive authority in that witnessing role. A robustly Christological hermeneutic positions scripture in its proper place as servant under Christ the Word:

> The object of faith is . . . the living, redeeming God incarnate in Jesus Christ, attested nowhere more decisively than in Holy Scripture. . . . The object of our faith is not the church or the Scriptures, not even our experience of Jesus Christ. It is Jesus Christ himself, but Christ testified to in Scripture and proclaimed by the church.[7]

The decisive but servant role of scripture in relation to Christ requires Baptists to operate with delicate theological balances, relating Christ to scripture without diminishing the proper authority of either:

> We have always honoured the Bible as the Spirit-inspired gift of God to his people, the reliable place where we can expect to hear the living Word of God. But we read it and we interpret it, with the help of the Holy Spirit, as witness to the one who is the Word of God in the fullest sense.[8]

To live under the rule of the Word is to practise a radical hermeneutic through which scripture bears final and decisive witness to Christ, and by which the living Christ, revealed in scripture and encountered in the community of faith, becomes the hermeneutical crux and criterion. 'The Bible is to be interpreted Christologically, with Christ as the key for interpreting the whole . . . Christ is the centre and makes sense of the whole.'[9]

For Baptists, then, it is Christ as revealed in the scriptures and present as the living Word amongst his people, who is the only and final norm of Christian faith. Living under the rule of the Word, means living under the lordship of the living Christ. But who Christ is, and what obedience to him implies, derives from scripture whose authority is therefore penultimate only to Christ:

> We must begin with Jesus Christ, who is the beginning and the end, the alpha and the omega. That is, our final authority is a person. It is not a book, or a creed, not even a basis of faith, but a person in whom God expresses God's self fully . . . . [It is] a Baptist conviction that ultimate authority is to be defined in terms of a person.[10]

On that basis Baptists affirm the freedom and competence of each believing community to interpret the scriptures under the guidance of the Holy Spirit, and to order its life in obedience to the Lord Jesus Christ in the light of such truth and understanding as it receives. Baptist spiritualities, though varying in emphasis and expression are characteristically Christ-centred, biblically informed, and corporately expressed in discipleship to Christ. Baptist life, personal and corporate, is formed and transformed under the rule of the Word as Christ and scripture. The final sections of this chapter will demonstrate Baptists using scripture, learning Christ through scripture and loving Christ within scripture, evidencing a balanced spirituality of discipleship and devotion.

2. Under the rule of the Word as Christ and scripture

Scripture is the gift of God's grace, the definitive authority as testimony and witness to Christ, and the medium through which the Holy Spirit brings the truth of Christ to bear on individual and community. The American Baptist theologian, E. Y. Mullins, described the relation of Christ to scripture in terms that recognized both the primacy of Christ, and the indispensability of scripture in knowing Christ:

> The Scriptures are the record of God's approach to man in Christ. These become to us the medium through which truth finds us, and without them Christ would inevitably pass into eclipse, and men would wander helpless, like a rudderless ship driven by tide and tempest.[11]

Mullins refused to concede a conflict between Christ and scripture, and in an important early work urged:

> Reason [cannot] be trusted to preserve the truth about Christ after the incarnation and completed revelation. . . . This is not to put the literature in the place of the Redeemer, but only to assert that the literature is a necessary medium for the transmission to us of a knowledge of him. Thus, the literature comes as the vehicle of objective truth about him and his salvation. . . . The relations between the literature [Bible] and the life [Christ] of which it is the expression must never be overlooked in defining the function of the Bible.[12]

According to Mullins' reasoning, Baptist existence under the rule of the Word requires that due weight be given to three controlling spiritual principles: corporate submission to Christ as revealed in scripture, a common commitment to the spiritual liberty of each believer, and shared responsibility to each other within the fellowship of believers seeking the mind of Christ. The tolerated tensions set up by these intersecting relational principles help define the distinctive dynamic of Baptist communities seeking to live together under the rule of the Word. As a covenanted community, engaging in conversation around the scriptures, paying attention to and seeking to be responsive to the Spirit, Baptists seek to create an overtly biblical ethos within which Christian experience, doctrinal convictions and ethical standards can be explored.

Self-definitions such as 'fellowship of believers', ' gathered community' or 'covenant people' rightly imply that individual Christians will find their essential spiritual context in the gatherings and meetings, the shared ministry and mission, of Christian community. In the gathered and covenanted community of believers each individual Christian enters an environment where doctrine and experience are explored and exposed to the corrective influences of corporate worship, biblical reflection, shared prayer, engagement in mission and pastoral care. And where such principles operate, the church lives as a community of shared insight, a body in living relationship to Christ, seeking together to articulate their experience and explore their faith within the frontiers of biblical revelation. Put more shortly, in exploring the implications of Christian belief and existence, Baptists appeal to 'the conscience of the church, inspired by the Spirit of God as a result of the study of the Bible.'[13]

A Baptist spirituality that seeks to live under the rule of the Word involves a self-conscious owning of the upper-case ambiguity at the end of the phrase 'under the rule of the Word'. The Word is Christ *and* scripture, but in that order.

> Absolute dependence upon Christ, the Sole and Sufficient Head of His Church, absolute dependence upon Christ as He reveals Himself by His Word and by His Spirit to His faithful people—that is the foundation of true Free-Churchmanship.[14]

Working out differences and disagreements in areas of doctrine, church practice, Christian ethics and expressions of spirituality must likewise take place under the rule of the Word, holding in balance the inter-related principles of Christ as norm, individual spiritual liberty and shared search for the mind of Christ. This initiates a dynamic and challenging process of dialogue within the context of shared worship, covenanted fellowship, corporate prayer as the body of Christ, and gathering in mutual submission under the authority of scripture. All this is the lived-out practice of individuals and community existing under the rule of the Word.

Exhorting his readers to use the Bible as a means to improve the vitality of their personal religion, Samuel Stennett urged:

> By the streams that flow from this pure fountain, the grace which is of divine implantation is watered and refreshed, and so flowers and becomes fruitful. Wherefore the frequent and serious use of the Bible is of the last importance. It should be read, meditated upon, treasured up in the heart and applied to practice. . . . Read it with a view to profit by

> it—endeavour to lay it up in your memory—in fine, pray to God to enable you to transcribe it into your life.[15]

Fruitfulness through serious use, application in practice, transcription into life: this is an unembarrassed utilitarian view of scripture. It understands the Bible as a divinely given means to a divinely ordained end, namely the maturing of the people of God under Christ, by the grace of God.

3. Believer and community under the rule of the Word

> Sola scriptura and soul competency are valid only as practised within the context of Christian community. Individual conscience is nurtured by the fellowship of the gathered community as the Holy Spirit works within the body of believers and as collectively and individually the Lordship of Christ is experienced. Scripture is an ecclesial document. Although read privately and individually, such private and individual reading is both disciplined and motivated through the interdependence of community.[16]

While recognizing legitimate community constraints and obligations, which exert control over individual decisions about doctrine and lifestyle choices, Baptists are equally protective of faith as personal trust and individual commitment. A spirituality that is initiated in free personal response to the gospel, but is nurtured in a fellowship of believers committed to covenant community as the body of Christ, brings the mind and conscience of the individual believer into essential conversation with the mind of the fellowship. In communities which place decisive significance upon evangelical experience as personal response to the Gospel, and which give this experience evidential value, these tensions become part of the discipline of living under the rule of the Word, as that Word is heard and understood within the local congregation. 'Free-churchmanship', that old-fashioned phrase passionately defined and defended by earlier Baptist apologists, serves as an awkward reminder that spiritual liberty is a defining characteristic of Baptist spirituality with a radical edge.

Spiritual liberty and freedom of conscience are more than core principles rooted in the history of nonconformity; they are grounded in a profoundly theological view of human personality as it encounters the gospel and is transformed by evangelical experience. To come under the gospel is to come 'under the rule of the Word', of Christ and scripture, so that the gospel-renewed personality recovers a sense of moral accountability to God and exercises faith as relationship between the individual soul and God the Saviour. As they pay attention to the scriptures as a sufficient revelation of God in Christ, believers encounter the Holy Spirit as guide, teacher and illuminator of those same scriptures. So they engage in worship as the free response of the whole personality to truth experienced in life, apprehended by the mind and gaining the consent of the will.

For such good theological reasons Baptists have historically affirmed the principle of the spiritual liberty of each person. But Christ is the interpretative key, giving substance to a Christ-centred and biblically measured spirituality. Spiritual liberty encourages neither theological reductionism nor vaguely defined piety. Personal loyalty to Christ as he is witnessed to by the scriptures, and that loyalty lived out in covenant fellowship with others, are experienced as disciplined constraints essential in every relationship of love. For Baptists, the principle of Christian liberty within the parameters of loyalty to Christ and the gospel, is fundamental to New Testament Christianity and personal spirituality. The freedom of the children of God is implied in the very nature of the gospel as the personal address of God to humanity through the living Word, the Lord Jesus Christ, incarnate, crucified, risen, and articulated in the apostolic testimony of scripture.

There is an important dialectic, then, between liberty in Christ and loyalty to Christ. In giving attention to this, a Baptist Christian is enabled to explore, apply and live out the gospel. There are inherent tensions in every local spiritual community where there is wide diversity of Christian experience, ethical insight and theological opinion, and where differing factions appeal to the same sources of spiritual authority. In such a situation, liberty in Christ, personally claimed and granted to others, and loyalty to Christ provide two spiritual principles between which individual and community seek to live under the rule of the Word. Loyalty to Christ is grateful and faithful obedience which will always limit the scope of liberty in Christ to that which is Christ-honouring; liberty in Christ is a risk-taking, glad freedom to love and serve Christ at all costs, constrained only by that same loyal love.

The Methodist Charles Wesley, always suspicious of dogmatic confessions and an apologist for direct experience of God biblically interpreted, points to the deep wound of love, the signature on the heart, that marks the Christian as belonging to Christ:

> Not from our creeds alone
> The doctrine we receive:
> Jehovah three in one,
> He gives us to believe:
> The God of truth Himself imparts,
> And writes His name upon our hearts.[17]

Wesley notwithstanding, while Baptists highly value spiritual experience, it does not carry unqualified authority. 'For [Baptists] Scripture is a sure, unchanging authority in contrast with human experience that is variegated, capricious and undependable.'[18] The Christological shape and content of experience confirms its evidential value. That which gives faith its conviction, which grasps the intellect, constrains the conscience and renews and redirects the will is the personal encounter with the living Christ and and surrender to him, learned through scripture and loved as encountered within scripture.

Article 69 of the Confession of Faith published after the death of John Smyth in 1612 affirms a principle of inclusive generosity at the heart of early Baptist church order which has not always been evident in the centuries since. The point is important for Baptist spirituality because it applies a powerful braking system to a spiritual theology in which either hardened individual opinion, or undue community pressure can be given oppressive legitimacy. This oppression can happen through appeal to a single expression of personal experience, or a single construal of Scriptural evidence. So the Confession affirms:

> That all penitent and faithful Christians are brethren in the communion of the outward church, wheresoever they live, by what name soever they are known, which in truth and zeal follow repentance and faith, though compassed with never so many ignorances and infirmities; and we salute them all with a holy kiss, being heartily grieved that we which follow after one faith, and one spirit, one Lord and one God, one body and one baptism, should be rent into so many sects and schisms; and that only for matters of less moment.[19]

True to such convictions Baptists argue that the fundamental doctrines of Christian faith are adequately safeguarded in the experience of the believing community only when it is seeking to be obedient to Christ, loyal to the scriptures and open to the guidance of the Holy Spirit within the local church, the body of Christ.

Generous welcome is based on core Baptist convictions. The originating and definitive source of Christian truth is Christ as revealed in scripture, encountered, apprehended, proclaimed and believed through the work of the Holy Spirit. The gospel of Jesus is woven into the textured fabric of a living Christian community, and is explored and explained in mission and ministry as each gathered community of believers scatters to witness to Christ and live in obedient discipleship to him. The meeting place between God and the human personality responding in trustful surrender is a sacred space, not to be trampled on by inquisitorial zeal for doctrinal formulation or an imposed uniformity of experience. The Word under whose rule the Christian community shapes its life, bears witness to a gospel whose scope is cosmic, which proclaims and celebrates a love that surpasses knowledge, and which is embedded in the eternal, infinite and ultimately baffling grace of God.

The rich variety among individuals' history, personality and experience, combined with the multiplicity of approaches open to the sovereign grace and redeeming love of God, make each believer's own personal relationship to Christ holy ground. In a Baptist ethos, how believers live out their commitment to follow Christ is governed by the call and command of Christ. That call and command comes home to their individual conscience by the laws of Christ as Christ himself is encountered, loved and known through scripture. It is also, however, shaped by the correctives and encouragements, the grace and the gift of a community which is sacramental in its capacity to mediate the reality of the grace and demand of Christ.

David Scholer thus strongly defends both the awkward diversity and the communal discipline that inform and influence Baptist understandings of scripture:

> We defend the freedom of persons to engage in interpretations that break community boundaries . . . or ones we think are uninformed, irresponsible, or even weird. But the freedom of interpretation that is in dynamic tension with any meaningful concept of biblical authority must be carried out within the triangular interaction of biblical authority, interpretative freedom, and the faith community's boundaries. To be sure, those boundaries are often unclear, may themselves be items for debate, may shift or change with time or circumstance, but are nevertheless part of the interpretive dilemma (or trilemma?) of responsible freedom.[20]

Living under the rule of Christ, and being submissive to the norm of scripture, has given rise amongst Baptists to a diversity of understandings about how scripture operates in the life of individual and community. In practice, how is the Bible to be read, interpreted and applied in the life of the individual? What is the relationship between the words of the text and the Word that became flesh? What is intended by the term 'Word of God' ? How do Baptists relate Christ to scripture? Is it Christ *through* scripture, Christ *within* scripture, Christ *before* scripture, even Christ *above* scripture? Each preposition placed between Christ and scripture has substantial theological force, representing a style of spirituality likely to be found somewhere on the Baptist historical and global spectrum.

The remainder of this chapter will explore several different, even contrasting approaches to scripture, from the mystical piety of sermons on the Song of Songs to scholarly commentary in contemporary biblical studies, from hymns long obsolete to preached biblical expositions which, with their unapologetic dependence on the biblical evangelical meta-narrative, fail most post-modern hermeneutic criteria. By drawing together such an eclectic selection of devotional testimony from a number of Baptist

Christians who have sought to live under the rule of the Word, it is possible to sense something of the original enthusiasm and spiritual passion with which they lived and performed their faith under the rule of the Word.

4. Learning Christ through scripture—discipleship

The Baptist poet, Anne Steele, was the first major female hymn-writer. She wrote a number of hymns extolling the efficacy of scripture as the source of Christ's instruction and as the medium through which Christ is encountered, known and loved. Still used in *Baptist Praise and Worship* today, her hymn 'Father of mercies in Thy word' illustrates the dependence of the Christian on scripture for a knowledge of Christ which comes from both learning and adoring, hearing and responding, to the voice of God through scripture.

In the hymn[21] there is both affective expression and a figurative, spiritual use of sense satisfaction in the relationship between reader, text and Christ. The 'free repast', 'sublimer sweets' and 'longing taste' suggest a banquet of 'heavenly peace', 'everlasting joys' and 'dear delight' for those who open the scripture. This is the Bible as sumptuous feast, as soul-satisfying nourishment, as the mediation of religious experience. The 'fair tree of knowledge' recalls the tree of the knowledge of good and evil (Genesis 2:17), but this is a supernatural tree, and the voice that is heard is not the serpent's. It is 'the Redeemer's welcome voice'. It is a free repast, without the dire expense of that previous eating from a tree of knowledge.

Father of mercies, in thy word
What endless glory shines?
Forever be thy name ador'd
For these celestial lines . . .

Here, the fair tree of knowledge grows
And yields a free repast,
Sublimer sweets than nature knows,
Invite the longing taste . . .

Here, the Redeemer's welcome voice,
Spreads heavenly peace around;
And life, and everlasting joys
Attend the blissful sound . . .

O may these heavenly pages be
My ever dear delight,
And still new beauties may I see,
And still increasing light.

Divine instructor, gracious Lord,
Be thou forever near,
Teach me to love thy sacred word,
And view my Saviour there.

Scripture is celebrated here as the source of the knowledge of God, and especially of Christ. But the 'Divine instructor' is invoked to teach not only knowledge as information, but knowledge as love, as willing dependence on the trusted Other who is 'forever near'. True knowledge is discipleship. Bible study is a learning process, but also a faith-deepening act of devotional search for the beloved—'teach me to love thy sacred word / and view my Saviour there'.

Two centuries later, another Baptist was wrestling with the intricacies of Johannine theological reflection on the relation of Christ to his disciples, and on the inner relations and outward works of Father, Son and Spirit in the economy of salvation. Beasley-Murray's commentary on the Gospel of John is written using the full range of historical-critical apparatus, conversant with the best academic scholarship. Scholarly criticism co-exists with an instinctive reverence for the integrity of the text, preventing forced harmonization and avoiding foregone theological conclusions. At one point, acknowledging the awkward questions raised by John 14 for systematic theologians, he insisted, 'If that sets a problem for the theologian it is necessary to resolve it through reflection on the text, not to interpret the text in the light of speculative theology.'[22] That is the scripture norm in action.

Throughout, the reader is guided through textual, contextual, historical and theological observations by a commentator alert to the one whom Anne Steele calls 'the Divine Instructor'. Beasley-Murray's attitude to biblical criticism was positive: 'Critical questions are matters of fact, to be investigated in a spirit of adventure not of fear. We need the guidance of the Spirit, not bludgeons to defend [the Bible].'[23] As an evangelical Christian, a Baptist, and a critical exegete,[24] Beasley-Murray's pastoral tone, and intentionally practical application of gospel to church is evident throughout. In his comment on the role of the Spirit as the interpreter of Jesus, he explained, '[The Paraclete] not only enables them to recall these things but to perceive their significance, and so he teaches the disciples to grasp the revelation of God brought by Jesus in its richness and profundity.'[25] The words of the Word are interpreted by the Spirit and made contemporary in the life of the church.

Beasley-Murray anticipated no difficulty for the modern church in appropriating John's eschatological perspective and applying it to contemporary challenges. He described the command to love one another as 'a direction to members of Christian churches to become fellowships of Christly love . . . Christians need love as much as anyone else . . . havens of deep and supportive love . . . [this is] mission by attraction, "centripetal" rather than "centrifugal.'[26]

The following longer quotation from this commentary exposes the unembarrassed hopefulness of a New Testament scholar who believes in the truth of the text, and in the Truth to whom the text bears witness. The careful exegete, by close study of grammar, syntax, literary genre and socio-historical background, reaches by a different route the reality the hymn writer intended by seeing 'new beauties' and the shining of 'endless glories'; here the 'increasing light' is of a post-Easter faith in the reality of the Christ who comes:

> To disciples shattered by the prospect of their Master's death and the disclosure of their own weakness, to churches which follow the crucified Messiah and experience the world's hostility formerly directed to him, and to Christians of later times confused by a secularism that sees no ground for faith or hope, the revelation . . . comes as the breath of heaven in an airless room. The prospect for the future . . . is of sharing

> in the joyous fellowship of the Father's house; the individual believer finds his goal in the perfected fellowship of redeemed humanity with the Son of God and his Father. But the journey to that future is by a way characterised by the Life of the Father's house, the expansive life of the coming glory scaled down to the dimensions of existence in this present world. Here the duality of perspective that binds the disciples in the Upper Room and the churches of the post-Easter period is clear; what to the disciples is a puzzling revelation of a future reunion with the Lord, becomes the foundation stone of the Church's relation to the Living Lord. Easter has happened! With it the life of the age to come has become the life of the Church today.[27]

Christ is learned through scripture, whether meditative poetry untutored in biblical criticism, or scholarly excavations in ancient languages and cultures. Either way the purpose of scripture is to point to Christ, that those who read may behold the glory of the Word made flesh, full of grace and truth. Through scripture the church learns of Christ, is renewed in hope, and lives the future now.

A different Baptist altogether was the Revd. John Gill, massively learned, soaked in biblical lore, high Calvinist in theology, Baptist pastor with a penchant for controversy and author of super-heavyweight theological tomes running to millions of words. 'As deeply as human sagacity, enlightened by grace, could penetrate, he went to the bottom of every thing he engaged in'.[28] For Gill the Bible was the rule of life, regulating all of life, intellectual, spiritual and practical:

> A sure, certain, and infallible rule to go by, with respect to things both to be believed and done: a rule they are (Gal. 6:16). And since they are of divine authority, and are perfect and plain, they are a sure rule, and to be depended on . . .The Scripture is the best interpreter of Scripture, or the Spirit of God therein . . . there is a private interpretation of Scripture, which every Christian may make, according to his ability and light; and there is a public one, by the preacher of the word; but both are subject to, and to be determined by the Scripture itself, which is the only certain and infallible rule of faith and practice.[29]

Scripture is a rule, however, because through its study each believer comes to a knowledge of God in Christ and develops a taste for spiritual things. There is a magnetic attraction of the soul to the 'personal and transcendent excellencies' of Christ, a maturing in love and faith for the One who is his own interpreter through scripture:

> Let us bless God for the scriptures, that we have such a way-mark to direct us, and point out unto us the way in which we should go; let us make use of them; let us search the scriptures daily and diligently, and the rather, since they testify of Christ, of his person, offices, of his doctrines and ordinances.[30]

Learning Christ through scripture involves meditative submission of heart and mind to the Spirit of Christ, and dedication of the spiritual affections to concentrate on, envisage, call to mind and memory, the glory of Christ.

> The Sacred Scriptures . . . are a sealed book to learned and unlearned men, destitute of the Spirit of Christ; only to be looked into so as to be understood by such who have their eyes enlightened, their understandings opened by Christ, as were the disciples; the scriptures are to be diligently searched into, and explored for the rich treasure that is in them . . .[31]

Gill could be a belligerent controversialist, an exhaustive (and exhausting) amasser of detailed proofs on fine points of doctrine, a preacher reluctant to overtly invite response to his preaching lest he interfere with the operations of sovereign grace. But in his descriptive prose when he was captivated by the glory of Christ's transcendent excellencies, he could write with a lucid spiritual passion. Enlightened eyes and opened understanding gave way to an enraptured appreciation of Christ.

> A lovely sight it is to see him by faith, in the glory and beauty of his person, and in the fullness of his grace; such a sight is spiritual, saving, assimilating, appropriating, very endearing, and very glorious and delightful.[32]

Each of these Baptist Christians—Steele, Beasley-Murray, Gill—based their use of scripture on their conviction that scripture points unerringly to Christ. The Bible is essential for the assimilation into the life of the believer, through the work of the illuminating Spirit, of all that is to be learned of Christ the Word as he is encountered through scripture. In the school of Christ lifelong learning in discipleship through study of scripture is never an end in itself. It urges towards a deepening and maturing of Christian character under the rule of the Word, so that accumulated spiritual knowledge becomes transforming truth, experienced, practiced and fuelled by devotionally enriched religious affections. To learn Christ is to love him, and through loving him to learn more.

5. Loving Christ within Scripture—devotion

John Gill was quite clear that the nature and goal of Christian learning, and knowledge of Christ, is not 'mere notional speculative knowledge', but rather

> Spiritual and experimental knowledge of God . . . which leads men to mind and savour spiritual things. This is knowledge which is attended with faith in God as a covenant-God in Christ; it is fiducial knowledge, such as know his name put their trust in him . . . and such knowledge always includes in it love to God and the most cordial affection for him.[33]

In his exposition of the Song of Solomon, Gill demonstrates the heights and depths of 'experimental knowledge', and a tireless capacity for expressing 'the most cordial affection for Christ'. Like other eighteenth century evangelicals, including Anne Steele, Charles Wesley and John Newton, Gill used scripture not only as food for thought, but as fuel for imaginative meditation on his personal experience of Christ, and that of his hearers Sunday by Sunday. And that most enigmatic of scriptures, the Song of Solomon, he expounded and creatively exploited as a means of learning and extolling the loveliness of Christ.

Gill is not alone in his fascination with the Song of Solomon as a repository of spiritual imagery and imaginative possibility, which when preached with a Christological hermeneutic, are transmuted into a powerful appeal to deep and evocative religious instincts of union and communion with God.[34] Spurgeon's opinion of Gill is noteworthy, if only because it explains my decision to examine Spurgeon's use of the Song, instead of Gill's.

> Probably no man since Gill's days has at all equalled him in the matter of Rabbinical learning. Say what you will about that lore, it has its value: of course, a man has to rake among perfect dunghills and dust heaps, but there are a few jewels which the world could not afford to miss. Gill was a master cinder sifter among the Targums, the Talmuds, the Mishna, and the Gemara .... [When preaching] his frequent method of animadversion is, 'This text does not mean this', nobody ever thought it did; 'It does not mean that', only two or three heretics ever imagined it did; and again it does not mean a third thing, or a fourth, or a fifth, or a sixth absurdity; but at last he thinks it does mean so-and-so, and tells you so in a methodical, sermon like manner. This is an easy method, gentlemen, of filling up the time, if you are ever short of heads for a sermon.[35]

By contrast, Spurgeon's sermons on the Song are vivid examples of how scripture in the hands of a skilled rhetorician with a natural gift for homiletic theatre evoked powerful affective responses in a Victorian Baptist congregation. Spurgeon was deeply suspicious of advanced higher criticism and held that the Bible was the very Word of God which on every page pointed to Christ, and on few pages more telling in the exactness and extravagance of their reference to Christ than that 'most Holy Place' the Song of Solomon.

The Song provided Spurgeon with a vocabulary, grammar and syntax of praise to Christ, with sensuous and mystical imagery woven into speech of adoration and grateful love, enabling him to use the potent symbolism of human intimacy and communion as a figurative portrayal of the love affair between Christ and church.

> 'He is altogether lovely'. 'He is altogether'—not beautiful, nor admirable,—but 'lovely.' All His beauties are loving beauties towards us, and beauties which draw our hearts towards Him in humble love. He charms us, not by a cold loveliness, but by a living loveliness, which wins our hearts. His is an approachable beauty, which not only overpowers us with its glory, but holds us captive by its charms. He has within Himself an unquenchable flame of love, which sets our soul on fire. He is all love, and all the love in the world is less than His . . . It is a torrent which sweeps all before it when its founts break forth within the soul. It is a Gulf Stream in which all icebergs melt. . . .[36]

Spurgeon disliked the slippery terminology of mysticism; but sermons like this on the Song of Solomon are remarkable examples of imaginative scriptural allusion, soaked in Victorian sentiment and powered by the forceful rhetoric of a preacher whose vision of Christ was majestic in its range, magnetic in its intensity, and yes, mystical in its felt reality for preacher and hearer.

Sermon titles such as 'The Spiced Wine of my Pomegranates', 'Fragrant Spices from the Mountains of Myrrh' and 'Paved with love', indicate how a fertile imagination takes the love symbolism of the Song and unhesitatingly finds in them, with no sense of incongruity, references to divine love and the divine loveliness. Much of Spurgeon's rhetorical power was generated by an imagination incapable of recognizing hyperbole in the speech of praise:

> God intends to describe him and set him forth one day. He is waiting patiently, for patience is part of Christ's character; and God is setting forth the patience of Christ in the patient waiting. . . . The whole earth will one day be sweet with the praise of Jesus. Earth, did I say? This alabaster box of Christ's sweetness has too much fragrance in it for the world to keep it all to itself; the sweetness of our Lord's person will rise above the stars, and perfume worlds unknown. It will fill heaven itself. . . . The cycles of eternity as they revolve shall only confirm the statement of the blood-redeemed that he is altogether lovely. . . .[37]

While Spurgeon's spiritual passion is everywhere evident in his use of these texts, it is still brought under the constraints of a Reformed theology. The ecstatic language of love is framed in Calvinistic theology and Pauline terminology. It is the combination of mystical vision, biblical allusion, popular rhetoric and Evangelical Reformed theology, that raises some of these sermons to a level of spiritual power equal to other devotional treatments of the Song.

> Study to know the value of His favours . . . they are every one of them so costly, that, had all heaven been drained of treasure, apart from the precious offering of the Redeemer, it could not have purchased so much as the least of His benefits. . . . When you are enabled to see yourself as clothed in the imputed righteousness of Jesus, admire the profusion of precious things of which your robe is made. Think how many times the Man of sorrows wearied Himself at that loom of obedience in which He wove that matchless garment; and reckon, if you can, how many worlds of merit were cast into the fabric at every throw of the shuttle![38]

The range of emotional and spiritual passion evident in the address to Christ, the diversity of image and symbol employed to depict the loveliness of Christ, the rhetorical virtuosity of a preacher creating the emotional and conceptual context for spiritual experience; these are characteristics of sermons which were vehicles for a powerful devotional Christology. This is scripture used as a means to seeing, knowing, adoring and loving the Christ experienced in the heart and in the worship of a Baptist community. In the sermon 'Paved with Love' the preacher's insistent closing exhortation is 'Look'. Christ is seen in scripture: to see Christ is to love Him; to love Him and be loved by Him, that is to live under the rule of the Word.

> Of my life I can and must say, 'the interior thereof has been paved with love.' Look at the tessellated pavement of love beneath your feet for a moment. Do you see the Father's love—that golden mass of uncreated love, for the Father himself loves you!

> Look at Jesus' love, another diamond pavement beneath your foot—Jesus loved you to the death, with a love that many waters could not quench, nor floods drown!
>
> Look at those delightful embroideries from the divine needle, the precious promises! A thousand promises there are, but they are all love! Look down and see how all the attributes of God are engaged for you, but they are all in league with love! Look, then, at all the providences of God towards you, at all the exercises of His grace in your heart, and you will see many and strange colours of varied beauty, all blending in one wondrous pattern of deep, unsearchable love![39]

For George Beasley-Murray, however, to live under the rule of the Word meant dealing with the Bible in an altogether different way. As biblical scholar, pastor and Baptist Christian he sought an inner coordination of values and goals which informed a responsible approach to the interpretation and practice of Scripture: intellectual integrity in matters of truth and criticism, pastoral application of biblical learning to contemporary experience, and responsible freedom of conscience within the covenanted fellowship of Baptist community.

In Beasley-Murray's handling of the Bible the connection was strong between his scholarship and his faith, between learning of Jesus through Scripture, using the tools of criticism, and loving Jesus as encountered through Scripture and preached in the church. In the Preface to *Jesus and the Kingdom of God*, he urged sustained study of the foundation documents of Christian faith as a means of 'attention to Jesus':

> The length of the work is a reflection of the complexity and profundity of the instruction of Jesus. The concentration of thought in few words that characterises his sayings eludes cursory examination. . . . Prolonged meditation on the teaching of Jesus concerning the theme that dominated his life produces a remarkably consistent image. To provide an opportunity for such attention to Jesus is the aim of this book.[40]

Prolonged meditation, and paying attention to the teaching of Jesus, are the intellectual and spiritual postures of one seeking to live under the rule of the Word, while through his study of Scripture enabling others to do the same. Near the end of this detailed exegesis of the mind of Jesus concerning the kingdom of God, concluding his study of Mark 13, he indicates the inner attitudes of one who was expert in the eschatology of the New Testament, and who refused to be drawn into those speculative vagaries which give eschatology a bad name and spawn best-selling doomsday scenarios.[41] 'The end is near, but incalculable, and liable to come as a surprise; consequently, all must be on the alert. Essentially that means readiness for God at every moment in a life of faith and Christian service'.[42] Alert readiness and a life of trusting service, following after Christ and looking towards a Christ-focused future, combines with close study of the sacred text; as a result, he moves through knowledge gained to an inner re-orientation towards Christ and his coming. Learning and devotion coalesce.

The choice of a contemporary New Testament scholar as an example of a Baptist seeking to live under the rule of the Word could suggest an unhelpfully élitist interest in the more intellectually rarefied expressions of faith. But that would be to overlook the vocational cost and intentional discipleship that underlie and inform some of the best Baptist biblical scholarship. Near the end of his life, in 1999, Beasley-Murray gave the address to the graduating students of Spurgeon's College. In it he revealed something of his own understanding of his academic work in biblical studies and preaching, and its personal cost. Referring to the account of P.T. Forsyth's total exhaustion after hard wrestling with theological complexities, he went on:

> This surely represents the theologian's counterpart to the sacrificial toils which have been rendered to the Lord through the ages by men and women who are prepared to feel the weight of the cross as well as to preach it. And this, I believe, is the spirit demanded of all Christ's servants, whether they are in the heart of the jungle or in the quieter paths of a theological college or in a suburban pastorate. It is the costly response of the man or woman of God to the 'costly grace' of the Redeemer. Intelligence without it is like tongues and prophecy and miracle-working faith without love—nothing, absolutely nothing.[43]

To live under the rule of the Word, as Christ and scripture, is to live in response to the love of God. Quoting P.T. Forsyth, as always with approval, on the last page of *Jesus and the Kingdom of God*, Beasley-Murray sums up what it means to live the cross-centred life, under the rule of Christ, in the light of the resurrection, and facing God's future hopefully.

> 'The Christian revelation is not just God is love, but God's love is omnipotent.' It is precisely this that the cross, resurrection and parousia of Jesus Christ our Lord proclaim and bring to actuality, for in these deeds the revelation of God reaches its perfection. And that revelation conveys the promise of eternal good.
>
> In such faith the Evanston Assembly of the World Council of Churches concluded its message to the churches throughout the world, a message with which I concur: 'We do not know what is coming to us. But we know who is coming. It is he who meets us every day and who will meet us at the end—Jesus Christ our Lord'.[44]

The New Testament scholar immersed in Synoptic texts, Johannine theology, early Christian eschatology and a plethora of studies necessary for modern critical study of ancient texts, at first glance seems to have little in common with an eighteenth-century single woman, tragically bereaved, whose hymns reveal her feelings and faith with disconcerting emotional frankness. But Anne Steele and George Beasley-Murray were both Baptists. They both worked out their own spirituality in dialogue with Scripture, and as disciples following after Christ, within the Baptist tradition, they sought to learn and love Christ through exposure of heart and mind to Scripture.

Several features characterize the hymns of Anne Steele: an honest and accurate measurement of her inner spiritual climate, her ability to tell her evangelical experiences in theologically and emotionally charged language, and an instinctive reliance on scripture to interpret these in terms of her relation to Christ. 'Desiring to know and love Him more'[45] is one of Anne Steele's most accomplished hymns. In it she exults in the infinite capacities of Christ to comfort her and restore her waning confidence in the love of God and the goodness of life.

This hymn is a good example of how scripture becomes a means of deepening devotion to Christ. The first two verses are suffused with positive feelings of enjoyment, engendering a mood of anticipation, and evoking a prayer for revelation, so that unveiled beauty will deepen and increase love. 'Thy glory o'er creation shines' leads the reader to assume a celebration of creation as the revelation of God, but it is in the 'sacred word', 'in fairer brighter lines', that unveiled beauty is seen; then in a typically abrupt change of mood attention is fixed on 'My bleeding dying Lord'.

Thou lovely source of true delight,
Whom I unseen adore,
Unveil thy beauties to my sight,
That I might love thee more.

Thy glory o'er creation shines;
But in thy sacred word
I read in fairer, brighter lines,
My bleeding, dying Lord.

The next verse describes how "tis here', that is 'in thy sacred word', that low spirits, guilt and sorrow are countered with 'cheering beams of hope'. 'But ah, too soon . . . gloomy fears rise dark between'—between what and what, or who and whom? No explanation is given. Whether it is guilt, anxiety, depression, resentment or any number of negative feelings turned inward—whatever the cause, true delight has turned to complaint.

'Tis here, whene'er my comforts droop,
And sin and sorrow rise,
Thy love, with cheering beams of hope,
My fainting heart supplies.

But ah, too soon the pleasing scene
Is clouded o'er with pain;

My gloomy fears rise dark between,
And I again complain.

That last word, 'complain', is immediately followed by a threefold description of the loving and life-giving Jesus, who is invoked to dawn on the soul and dispel the gloomy fears of darkness. Strong verbs are used: the invocation 'Oh come!' is followed by a third line in which the verbal phrase 'break . . . through' is actually broken through with the word 'radiant', like the sun splitting clouds. Just so fears are chased away.

Jesus, my Lord, my life, my light,
Oh come with blissful ray
Break radiant through the shades of night,
And chase my fears away.

The sacred written Word is a source of delight and comfort, but the benefits are transient; life circumstances, inner changes of mood and spirit, soon interrupt the meditative reverie anticipated at the start. Only 'Jesus, my Lord, my life, my light' can enrapture the soul with the wonders of his love—and even then the full glory awaits the final unveiling 'above'. The sacred Word is what is available now, and through it the mediated presence of Christ breaking radiantly through as the soul is captivated by 'the wonders of thy love'.

Then shall my soul with rapture trace
The wonders of thy love;
But the full glories of thy face
Are only known above.

The hymn describes the relationship between Jesus and the writer using strong emotional words—love, rapture, delight. The radiant light dispels obscuring darkness and makes it possible to trace the wonders of divine love. The last verse plays a literary trick on the reader: the expected rhyming counterpart of 'trace' in the Evangelical thesaurus would be 'grace', but what will come to full recognition in heaven will be Jesus' 'face'. For now the vision is through a glass dimly, but then, face to face.

Jesus as life-giving light, and the exclusive focus of the soul's love, is expressed in a light-hearted, playful mood in Steele's hymn 'Christ the Christian's Life'. Through meditation the attention of the soul is fixed on the exalted Jesus in heaven:

There Jesus lives (transporting name!)
Jesus inspir'd the sacred flame,
And gave devotion wings;
With heaven-attracted flight she soar'd,
The realms of happiness explor'd
And smil'd, and pitied kings.[46]

Her hymn on John 17.24 renders into devotional verse what Beasley-Murray calls the 'ultimate horizons of the perfected kingdom which his Parousia will make possible.'[47] Through deep reflection on scripture, Steele provides an alternative engagement with the text, an experiential and emotional exegesis of the soul's 'ultimate horizons', the evangelical's beatific vision:

There shall our heart no more complain,
Nor sin prevail, nor grace decay;
But perfect joy forever reign,
One glorious, undeclining day.

There shall we see thy lovely face
And chang'd to purity divine,
Partake the splendours of the place
And in thy glorious likeness shine.[48]

6. Baptists, Christ and Scripture

Baptist devotion to Christ mediated through scripture takes a multitude of forms, as varied as the personalities and experiences of those who find Christ in and through scripture. Consciously or unconsciously, they live their faith within the conceptual framework of a Christ-centred hermeneutic that both stimulates their religious affections and defines their

Christian existence. The Baptists studied in this essay exemplify, in very different ways, what it meant for them to live under the rule of the Word, to learn of and to love the Christ encountered within scripture.

However the doctrine of scripture is construed, and allowing for wide variation, Baptists highly honour scripture and accord it not only privileged but primary authority as witness to and interpreter of Christ. As rule of life, scripture is God's gracious providential gift, illumined and opened by the Spirit who teaches the things of Christ. As witness to Christ, scripture is received by the church as its story, past present and future, an unfolding drama of redemption into which the church is drawn as the community of those called to follow Christ. As guidebook for those who seek the kingdom in covenant with each other and with God it is the norm for its life together as through worship, prayer and service, they discern the mind of Christ, as a community under the rule of the Word.

Baptist biblicism is energized by a deep reverence for the sacred text, an expectation that through reading, studying, hearing and reflecting on scripture, Christ is learned and known. The devotional use of scripture in deepening love for Christ, in pursuing the quest for holiness, in seeking guidance in the practicalities of following Christ, is a spiritual discipline shared across the Christian tradition. But in the context of a Baptist community, concentration on, and submission to Scripture, interacts with a network of other spiritual principles, which together create a distinctive spiritual ethos.

How Baptists relate Christ to scripture gives rise to spiritualities both unified and diverse. One Baptist theologian acknowledges, 'In general, Baptists identify scripture as the supreme earthly source of authority';[49] another points to Baptists' 'epistemological lodgement in the Scriptures.'[50] Each preposition placed between 'Christ' and 'scripture' exerts a substantial theological and spiritual qualification of how Christ and scripture operate as the Word under whose authority each Christian and each church lives its life. However Baptist identity is expressed, Baptist ecclesiology and spiritual theology presuppose the sole and absolute authority of Christ and the supreme authority of the scripture through which Christ is revealed.

In the practice of Baptist Christians, and in their devotional commitment to Christ and scripture, the use of the Bible supports several ways of aligning Christ and scripture. Insofar as they are seeking to live under the rule of the Word, they approach scripture believing that there they will learn of Christ, encounter Christ and deepen their love and trust in Christ the Word of God. Allowing for differing emphases and styles of spirituality, for each of the Baptists considered above Christ is the interpretive key of scripture. So we find the range of prepositions: as Word of God Christ is mediated *through* scripture; as the content of God's revelation Christ is discovered and encountered *within* scripture; as God manifest in the flesh Christ pre-exists and is therefore *before* scripture; as the One who has sole and absolute authority as author and content, Christ is *above* Scripture.

In their use of the Bible, Baptists did not always feel compelled to indulge in fine distinctions between Christ and scripture, nor anxiously differentiate between the 'original' or 'derivative' authority of scripture, nor sense the potential for conflict of interests between individual spiritual liberty and the covenanted community of believers. But in their different ways, arising from their personal experience of Christ, they believed that Christ, the living personal Lord and Saviour, is to be discovered through scripture in the lifelong learning of discipleship, and as encountered within scripture, to be loved with passionate devotion. Consequently it was for them, and for all Baptists, an *a priori* assumption that the Bible is uniquely and essentially authoritative in communicating the reality of the living Word. They are all lovers of Christ and scripture, readers and prayers of the sacred text, listeners and lifelong learners in the school of Christ, actors and performers in the unfolding drama of redemption, as they seek to live under the rule of the Word.

Notes

[1] 'A Confessional Statement', *American Baptist Quarterly*, 6/2 (1987), p. 62.

[2] See Steven R. Harmon, *Towards Baptist Catholicity. Essays on Tradition and the Baptist Vision* (Carlisle: Paternoster, 2006), p. 28: 'They evidenced a radical biblicism in their copious prooftexting of confessional statements with parenthetical and biblical references.'

[3] Paul Beasley-Murray, *Radical Believers* (London: Baptist Publications, 1992), p. 121.

[4] G. F. Nuttall, *Congregationalists and Creeds* (London: Epworth Press, 1967), p. 7.

[5] Nuttall, *Congregationalists and Creeds*, p. 7.

[6] The Constitution of the Baptist Union of Great Britain, Article III.1.

[7] Donald Bloesch, *Theology of Word and Spirit. Authority and Method in Theology* (Exeter: Paternoster, 1992), pp. 61, 39. See further pp. 118-25, 255-56.

[8] Richard L. Kidd (ed.), *Something to Declare: A Study of the Declaration of Principle of the Baptist Union of Great Britain* (Oxford: Whitley Publications, 1996), p. 29.

[9] Nigel G. Wright, *New Baptists, New Agenda* (Carlisle: Paternoster, 2002), pp. 22-3.

[10] Paul S. Fiddes, *Tracks and Traces. Baptist Identity in Church and Theology* (Carlisle: Paternoster, 2003), pp. 50-51, 58.

[11] C. Freeman, J. W. McClendon, C. R. V. da Silva (eds), *Baptist Roots. A Reader in the Theology of a Christian People* (Valley Forge: Judson Press, 1999), pp. 282, 288.

[12] E. Y. Mullins, *Freedom and Authority in Religion* (Philadelphia: Griffith & Rowland Press, 1913), pp. 350-2.

[13] Ernest Payne, *The Fellowship of Believers*. Second Edition (London: Carey Press, 1952), p. 19.

[14] Henry Cook, *The Why of Our Faith*. Third Edition (London: Carey Press, 1947), p. 75.

[15] Samuel Stennett, *Discourses on Personal Religion* (London: Richie, 1801), pp. 143-4.

[16] 'American Baptists: A Unifying Vision', *American Baptist Quarterly*, 6/2 (1987), p. 83.

[17] J. E. Rattenbury, *The Evangelical Doctrines of Charles Wesley's Hymns* (London: Epworth, 1941), p. 149.

[18] William H. Brackney, *Baptists in North America* (Oxford: Blackwell, 2006), p. 4.

[19] R. C. Walton, *The Gathered Community* (London: Carey Press, 1946), pp. 72-3.

[20] David Scholer, 'The Authority of the Bible and Private Interpretation', in Everett C. Goodwin (ed.) *Baptists in the Balance* (Valley Forge: Judson Press, 1997), p. 190.

[21] Anne Steele, *Hymns, Psalms and Poems* (London: Daniel Sedgwick, 1863), pp. 36-8. Also included in: *Baptist Praise and Worship* (Oxford: Oxford University Press, 1991), pp. 66-7.

[22] George Beasley-Murray, *John*. Word Biblical Commentary (Waco: Word Publishers, 1987), pp. 260-61.

[23] Paul Beasley-Murray, *Fearless for Truth. A Personal Portrait of the Life of George Beasley-Murray* (Carlisle: Paternoster, 2002), p. 174.

[24] While Principal of Spurgeon's College, Beasley-Murray was responsible for the translation of Bultmann's celebrated commentary on *John*, for many a disconcerting example of his openness to the best insights of modern critical exegesis.

[25] Beasley-Murray, *John*, p. 261.

[26] Beasley-Murray, *John*, pp. 263-4.

[27] Beasley-Murray, *John*, p. 264.

[28] M. A. G. Haykin, (ed.), *The Life and Thought of John Gill. 1697-1771* (Leiden: Brill, 1997), p. 116.

[29] John Gill, *Complete Body of Doctrinal and Practical Divinity* (1770). *A New Edition in Two Volumes* (Grand Rapids: Baker Book House, 1978 = London: 1795 repr. 1839), Vol. I, ch. 2, p. 32.

[30] John Gill, *A Collection of Sermons and Tracts in Two Volumes* (London: George Keith, 1773), Vol. II, Sermon XVI 'The Scriptures: the Only Guide in Matters of Religion', p. 496.

[31] Gill, *Sermons and Tracts*, Vol. II, Sermon XXXIX, 'The Doctrine of the Cherubim Opened and Explained', p. 43.

[32] John Gill, An *Exposition of the Books of the Prophets of the Old Testament* (London: George Keith, 1757), on Isaiah 6:5, p. 33.

[33] Haykin, *John Gill*, p. 199.

[34] Prior to Gill, Protestant treatments included selected sermons by John Flavel and Richard Sibbes, and full expositions by James Durham and John Cotton. Samuel Rutherford's *Letters* are heavily laced with the love language and imagery of the Song addressed to Christ.

[35] C. H. Spurgeon, *Commenting and Commentaries* (Edinburgh: Banner of Truth, 1969), p. 9.

[36] C. H. Spurgeon, *Till He Come* (Tain: Focus Publications, 1989), pp. 101-2.

[37] C. H. Spurgeon, *The Most Holy Place* (Fearn: Christian Focus Publications, 1996), pp. 460-1.

[38] Spurgeon, *Till He Come*, pp. 130-1.

[39] Spurgeon, *Most Holy Place,* p. 290.

[40] George Beasley-Murray, *Jesus and the Kingdom of God* (Grand Rapids: Eerdmans, 1986), p. x.

[41] See George Beasley-Murray, *Jesus and the Last Days* (Peabody: Hendrickson, 1993), a benchmark study of Mark 13.

[42] Beasley-Murray, *Jesus and the Kingdom of God*, p. 337.

[43] Beasley-Murray, *Fearless for Truth*, pp. 202-3.

[44] Beasley-Murray, *Jesus and the Kingdom of God*, p. 344.

[45] Steele, *Hymns, Psalms and Poems*, pp. 101-2.

[46] Steele, *Hymns, Psalms and Poems,* p. 123.

[47] Beasley-Murray, *John*, p. 305.

[48] Anne Steele, *Hymns, Psalms and Poems*, p. 103.

[49] Harmon, *Baptist Catholicity,* p. 28.

[50] Brackney, *Baptists in North America*, p. 6.

6
Spirituality in Everyday Life: the View from the Table

John Weaver

1. Spirituality and daily life

Worship is the whole of life, as the Apostle Paul reminds us: 'present your bodies as a living sacrifice . . . which is your spiritual worship' (Romans 12:1-2). Worship is not restricted to what happens in church. We must make all the connections between faith and life, and faith and work, and recognize that discipleship is full-time ministry for all Christians.[1]

'Spirituality' has similarly wide scope. Paul Fiddes remarks in the introduction to this book that it is a slippery term, and it seems to be given a whole range of meanings by its use in the literature. But this capaciousness is because Christian spirituality concerns the living out of the encounter with Jesus Christ. It refers to the way in which the Christian life is understood and the explicitly devotional practices which have been developed to foster and sustain that relationship with Christ. Christian spirituality may be thus understood as the way in which Christian individuals or groups aim to deepen their experience of God, or as Brother Lawrence (c.1605-1691) wrote, 'to practise the presence of God: the best rule of holy life.' I find the definition proposed by William Stringfellow in *The Politics of Spirituality* to be helpful:

> Whatever else may be affirmed about a spirituality which has a biblical precedent and style, spiritual maturity or spiritual fulfilment necessarily involves the whole person—body, mind and soul, place, relationships—in connection with the whole of creation throughout the era of time. Biblical spirituality encompasses the whole person in the totality of existence in the world, not some fragment or scrap or incident of a person.[2]

It is this definition that best sums up the spirituality that I believe is encompassed by our celebration of the Lord's Supper, which is the main theme of this chapter. In the Supper we are exploring our relationship with God through Christ, our relationship with each other in the presence of the Holy Spirit, and our relationship with the world where, as Paul Fiddes suggests, we share in the *perichoresis* (mutual indwelling) of the triune God.[3]

All this is a matter of discipleship. Many Christians have a surprising ability to live in two worlds: the private world of faith and the public world of work and daily life. To follow Christ in our daily lives involves asking God questions of each and every part of our lives. Bringing the private and public worlds together is the main task facing the church as it seeks to engage with the whole of life in the mission of Christ. There can be a flight from reason, where worship becomes a welcome respite from a tough and demanding world, and we deny God the opportunity to encounter us in the concerns of our life in the world: to challenge, direct, forgive, and bring peace.

In today's complex world, religious faith, taken as a whole, serves as a welcome oasis for many people. John Hull has rightly suggested that it may be valued 'precisely because there one can escape from the problems and demands which crowd in upon us from the newspapers and the television.'[4] He is right to note that, for many people home and church are havens from the confusion of a post-modern world. While Monday to Friday are spent among the pressures and questions of a technological world with its pluralistic values and beliefs, Saturday is spent in the safe haven of home, and Sunday in the safe haven of the church.

We cannot live without meaning and purpose. Christian discipleship is a full-time occupation, seven days a week. The Christian faith needs to relate to every part of our lives, for there is no part of our lives with which God is not involved. The good news is that God is able to transform every part of our existence. The first sign in the Gospel according to John is of Jesus who transforms water into wine.[5] He can transform our watery existence into the richness of the life redeemed through his blood. An important aspect of the 'wholeness' of Christian spirituality is that we correlate our theological beliefs with our personal experience. Our experience is informed by theological reflection, which is a central part of the correlation process. Spirituality emerges from a creative and dynamic synthesis of faith and life, which has to be worked out through a commitment to live out Christian discipleship actively, radically and with integrity.

This discipleship begins in the focus of baptism, as the once-for-all participation in the death and resurrection of Christ—dead to sin, dead to self, rising to new life in the power of the Spirit, as described in Romans 6:1-14. In this passage Paul uses baptism as an illustration of Christian commitment, of living the Christian life, since he is assuming that all Christians are baptized (cf. 1 Corinthians 12:13). The Christian life is rooted in participation in the events of Golgotha and Easter Day through union with Christ. Being joined to Christ we have received a death sentence on the old way of life and we seek grace for a new existence and conduct. Baptism is thus a sacrament of everyday life. Here Paul Fiddes helpfully notes that

> Believers' baptism underlines a final allegiance to Christ alone, though also affirming that this allegiance is not worked out as a private individual, but within the whole polis or human community. Believers' baptism is entrance to church membership, which among Baptists . . . is always understood to carry responsibilities of active discipleship.[6]

Our commitment to the world of the everyday, begun in baptism, is continued in our celebration of the Lord's Supper, which has both an individual and a corporate dimension. We often refer to those who share our life journey as companions. The origin of the word 'companion' is to be found in the Latin words *cum* and *panus*, meaning 'with bread'. Our companions are those with whom we share our meals, with whom we break bread. At the time when the New Testament was written eating meals together was a common feature of most social groups, and the same basic features were present in both sacred and secular meals. Dennis Smith and Hal Taussig note that ancient banquets were characterized by:

- *Social bonding*: there is a special tie amongst the diners, celebrating their community and friendship.

- *Social obligation*: the meal brings ethical obligations of friendship, love, joy and pleasure between individuals; as group, there are obligations to serve the common good, and to edify each other with good conversation.
- *Social stratification*: this is defined by seating position at the table.
- *Social equality*: the meal tended to break down social barriers. 'The equality that lies at the heart of the ideal communal meal is also reflected in the Passover liturgy specification that the poor should recline equally at the table on this occasion and receive at least four cups of wine.'[7]

Smith and Taussig suggest that 1 Corinthians 11, for example, describes just such a banquet pattern.

In a previous chapter, Paul Fiddes writes of the participants' awareness of each other, their attention to each other, as a central part of the Baptist experience of the Lord's Supper. It seems to me that there is much to re-discover in this experience of celebrating a meal where participation is in common, and the liturgy and ritual is actualized in the experience of both the individual and the community. With regard to the individual, the Supper offers:

- giving and receiving the peace: forgiveness and the presence of Christ
- receiving the elements
- re-making an individual covenant with God
- inward spiritual growth in Christ

For the community, the Supper offers:

- giving and receiving the peace: reconciliation with each other
- testimony to the gospel
- re-making the covenant to 'walk together and watch over each other in love'
- outward spirituality through mission and discipleship (life and work)

As individuals and as community we make our response to God's grace, giving ourselves wholly. God moves towards us in Christ, and we respond to God, but the first movement is always from God. That of God, which is given to me in Christ, is re-appropriated in the Lord's Supper.

2. Attention to the body of Christ at the Supper

There is a great deal of importance in telling each other the story which is celebrated through the Lord's Supper. We move away from individualism and 'what I get out of church', to a recognition and understanding of the body of Christ. To make this clear, I want in a moment to bring together the celebration of the Lord's Supper and the church meeting as characteristics of true Christian community. Eleanor Kreider aptly describes an 'impulse toward commonality' which is expressed in the celebration of the Lord's Supper. She rightly asserts that joining together in worship is in stark contrast to the 'primary impulse of Western individualism.'[8]

(a) Going to the roots

We recognize from our Baptist forebears that the celebration of a community gathered by Christ is what unites and binds the members together as the body of Christ. The Anabaptists of the Radical Reformation in the sixteenth century were Christ-centred and gospel-centred. To learn from such groups the church today should avoid an exclusively Pauline diet, instead finding the stories of Jesus in the four Gospels as the hermeneutic key. The Anabaptist 'gathering church' is a dynamic community working together with others, hearing the voice of Jesus in the Bible, and then going and living that out in society.

The Anabaptist emphasis for church life is community. Keith Jones describes the basis of such communities as 'God gathering people together in communities of committed discipleship', where baptism marks the 'incorporation of that person into a faith community engaged in communal discipleship and sharing a particular missionary ideology.'[9] It is a 'gathering', not a 'gathered' church, not complete, but believers gathering together on their journey of discipleship. Anabaptists had their scholars, such as Balthasar Hubmaier, but these were part of the fellowship of believers, where all members had a valuable contribution to make.

It was important to find those, with a servant heart, who were able to enable the church community to develop its discipleship.

They were inclusive communities, who together searched for the mind of Christ. Jones suggests that such local Christian communities were defined in terms of orthopraxis:

> Holding fast in a local gathering church of believers to a Christocentric view of Scripture; being committed to the concept of the gathering church; holding fast with a biblical model of Baptism; and to the gathering community being the place for determining the mind of Christ and handling the disciplining of the faithful.[10]

They were a sacramental people who experienced the reality of Christ in the scriptures, through baptism and the Lord's Supper. Quoting from James McClendon, Keith Jones notes their two central distinctives, marked by two sacraments or ordinances. First there was discipleship, understood neither as a vocation for the few nor an esoteric discipline for adepts, but as the life transformed into service by the lordship of Jesus Christ. This was signified by believers' baptism. Second there was community—understood not as a privileged access to God or to sacred status, but as sharing together in a storied life of obedient service to and with Christ. This was signified by the Lord's Supper.[11]

The understanding of the Lord's Supper has varied, and still does vary, amongst Baptists. The Westminster Confession of Faith (1646), chapter XXIX, section VII states concerning the Eucharist:

> Worthy receivers, outwardly partaking of the visible elements in this sacrament, do then also inwardly by faith, really and indeed, yet not carnally and corporally, but spiritually, receive and feed upon Christ crucified, and all the benefits of his death: the body and blood of Christ being then not corporally or carnally in, with, or under the bread and wine; yet as really, but spiritually, present to the faith of believers in that ordinance, as the elements themselves are to their outward senses.[12]

Prior to this, John Smyth (1610) had spoken of the spiritual Supper which stirs up repentance and faith, but later on Baptists adopted two different views. There were Baptists who held the kind of sacramental belief represented by the Westminster Confession, especially those who stood in the Calvinistic tradition. The Particular Baptist Confession of 1677, for instance, repeats the section from the Westminster Confession virtually word for word, so affirming that believers 'spiritually receive and feed upon Christ crucified'.[13] In this succession, Robert Hall (1815) understood communicants to be partakers by faith of the body and blood of Christ, and C.H. Spurgeon (1855, 1888) understood the Supper as both the commemorative feast of Jesus' friends and as means of 'partaking in his body and blood, by faith, with all his benefits, to our spiritual nourishment, and growth in grace'. Alternatively, however, there were those who understood the Supper as essentially a memorial meal, such as John Sutcliffe (1800) and Alexander Maclaren (1884).

Eleanor Kreider suggests that strict 'memorialism' was a product of the Enlightenment rather than due to Zwingli to whom it is often attributed, and that the central problem for us today is rather different from the disputes of the past: it is that our view of communion is individualistic, narrow, and small. She poses the question: how can we reclaim the piety of early Christianity in which the presence of the risen Lord, at his table, engaged the whole of the community's life—individual, social, and material?[14]

Each generation has found fresh insights from the New Testament communities. The Spirit in every generation continues to bring forgiveness, healing and hope at the Lord's table. God, who is Spirit, reaches out to communicate with us through the bread and wine of the Supper. We receive forgiveness, joy, healing and reconciliation. The meaning of the cross is clearly seen as our worship proclaims the Lord's death, and Christ's own self-giving is mirrored in relationships within his church. Eleanor Kreider encourages churches to explore the themes of thanksgiving, feasting, sharing, reconciling, forgiving, healing, covenant, discipline, serving, and justice. Such exploration will shape our individual characters and the character of the church.

She challenges the church to recognize that the way we take communion makes a difference, for we act out or perform our communion theology. A key question is whether we partake only as individuals or also as a community. 'Dead ritual' is easy to spot, since a moribund rite is no substitute for reality; it can be seen, for example, in the breaking of bread and pouring of wine in a congregation of people whose lives are in no way broken for the world or poured out in love for their neighbours.[15] The language of ritual speaks most powerfully when it is deeply connected to the circumstances of people. In retelling the story of God's creating, redeeming and liberating love, we find that the Spirit is able to minister to our individual and community needs.

Similarly Smith and Taussig maintain that the early church did not have a set liturgy, and that the picture of the early church presents us with a variety of eucharistic practices, which can invite churches today to be in creative dialogue with their particular social and cultural settings. They challenge the church today in stating that

> The mix of social interaction and ritual in first-century meals directs the contemporary churches toward formats in which contemporary social and personal concerns can both shape and be integrated into worship. It provides a rationale and impulse for opening up obtuse and formulaic gestures to creative interplay with the issues of the particular communities and individuals.[16]

They rightly observe that we can include prayers for both the fellowship and the community, and that the table might contain pictures and artefacts that are appropriate to that particular moment in the congregation's life, alongside the bread and the wine.

Celebration of the Lord's Supper can be seen as both communicative and commemorative. First, the Supper communicates as a means of grace: that is, Christ is present, we are conjoined by the Spirit, and there is a renewal of our covenant with Christ and with each other. Donald Baillie helpfully asks if we are saved by faith or by the sacraments. His answer is: by neither, but by God, who saves us through faith and therefore partly by the sacraments that he uses to awaken and strengthen our faith.[17] Second, the Supper commemorates. There is remembrance and response to memory. We stand between memory and hope, between incarnation and consummation. Hope looks to the future, while memorial looks to the past, and we cry *Marana tha! Come Lord Jesus*, looking for a coming which is both present and eschatological.

Thus we are not celebrating with empty symbols, but ones which enable us to participate in the death and resurrection of Christ. We recognize this when we consider the Jewish understanding of the Passover, which in turn is reflected in the New Testament presentation of the Lord's Supper and of baptism (see 1 Corinthians 10 and also 1 Corinthians 6:12-20). To understand the connection, we need to think about the power of story.

(b) Sharing in a story

The community grows together as its members celebrate the Lord's Supper, recalling the story of the Jewish Passover and the story of Jesus' last meal with his disciples on the way to the cross. But then we recognize that each individual Christian's story is a part of this story as it reflects the activity of God in our lives. Out of the church's story comes the vision of the kingdom of God, what God wants to do and is able to do in lives that are open to his purposes. Given the reality of our sin, especially in terms of self-centredness, this vision of the kingdom is always 'not yet,' and this is a limiting factor in all our praxis. Yet American theologian and educationalist Thomas Groome is right to hold out the goal to us:

> In the community encounter between our own stories and the Story, between our own visions and the Vision, we can come to 'know God' in an experiential/reflective manner. It will be a praxis way of knowing that arises from our own praxis, from the praxis of our community of pilgrims in time, and from the praxis of God in history.[18]

The New Testament scholar C.F.D. Moule is right to state that the gospel is more than declaration, something to read and know; it is experience, and faith is a lived faith. God's unique action in Christ is not some 'dead and static thing,' it is the living God at work through the church as the body of Christ. The incarnation is a unique point in history, but 'if it is continuous with the People of God before it, then in some sense redemption must be continued with the Church after it.'[19]

Story is a vital ingredient in the Lord's Supper or Eucharist, and we recognize that it encompasses at least four stories:[20]

- *Story number one:* The Hebrew people make an exodus from Egypt, a journey to safety through the Reed Sea, which concludes with a covenant at Mount Sinai. The Israelites later remembered all of this at an annual celebration of being the people of God (Deuteronomy 16:1-4). It was this meal that Jesus celebrated with his disciples on that fateful Passover eve.
- *Story number two:* Twelve hundred years later, Jesus knowing that his life is coming to an end, celebrates one last festival meal of the people of God, with his close friends. It is Passover time, and they celebrate the Passover meal, recorded in Mark 14:22-26. Jesus gives new meaning to the Passover; it is a new covenant of forgiveness and love, which is in Christ and his death. We are to become people of this new covenant through becoming one with Jesus in his death and resurrection.
- *Story number three:* Twenty years have passed and as a result of the evangelistic ministry of Paul the gospel has reached Corinth. In obedience to Jesus' command at his last meal, the church everywhere celebrates the supper, often as a part of their fellowship together, and as part of a love feast. It marks their love for each other. Sadly, in Corinth, there are plenty of divisions and not much fellowship. Paul reaffirms the Lord's Supper through the words recorded in 1 Corinthians 11:23-29.
- *Story number four:* We are now part of this story. As we share the bread and wine, we participate in the death and resurrection of Christ; we die to self and rise to a new life of discipleship, in the power of the Holy Spirit. Our fellowship has its own story to tell, in expressing itself as a Christian community.

The development of a literary culture has removed much of the personal from the celebration—the communication of the story from one person to another. Placing the story in a book has tended to remove it from the drama of the liturgy. It has also led to individualism and debate, where everyone has their own interpretation. The gospel is no longer focused in a person but in a book. In some ways the institutional church has lost the emphasis on a living faith, and we need to rediscover the journeying, pilgrim church, which tells, listens to, and lives the ongoing story. Eucharist helps us to recover such story-telling, for this is the place where the story is retold, and re-enacted, and where the people enter into the story. Paul Fiddes reminds us that communities are formed by the stories they tell:

> Remembering the story allows us to encounter the same God who is present in the community in the past, in exodus, crucifixion and resurrection. In telling the story we encounter the crucified and risen Lord anew, and this forms the community as the representative of this Lord in the world.[21]

(c) Relating and offering in the Supper

As we participate in the Lord's Supper, so we also understand what it means to be the church. The meal is not only a matter of our personal spirituality and relationship with God, but also of our corporate spirituality as the 'body of Christ,' incarnate in the world.

Eleanor Kreider believes, along with the apostle Paul, that Christians must 'discern the body'—learning to perceive the meaning of their actions, and to catch the implications of their behaviour. There is a need for the church to recover a true sense of community and hospitality through sharing meals, which are transformed through acted memory by Christ's own presence and love. Kreider concludes[22] that 'it is in this table gathering that we become who we are—the true body of Christ in and for the world.' We recognize that the table fellowship, the celebration of the Lord's Supper, and the story we tell of God's sacrificial love are truly sacramental, in manifesting a community of God's people capable of love and demonstrating forgiveness through their shared lives.

We recognize that forgiveness and reconciliation should be an essential part of our understanding of the Lord's Supper (Matthew 5:23-24; 1 Corinthians 11:18; 2 Corinthians 5:17-18). As John de Gruchy puts it,

> the sacraments are communal acts of remembering and representing the Gospel narrative through dramatic actions, using material signs and symbols—water, bread and wine, and acts of peacemaking and reparation. The sacraments rightly understood and practised within the worship life of the church play a central role in shaping Christian community and its witness to God's reconciliation.[23]

The sacraments are a means of grace for healing and transformation, and for creating community. As we covenant together, we turn outward to the task of reconciliation that God has given us. Paul Fiddes portrays the elements as meeting places with God, which he describes as 'doors into the dance of *perichoresis* in God' and 'signs which enable us to participate in the drama of death and resurrection which is happening in the heart of God.'[24] But he goes on to stress that 'The real presence of Christ is manifested in the community of the church, as it becomes more truly the body of Christ broken for the life of the world.'[25]

God is present to us through faith and we bring our worship as an offering to God through faith. But what can we bring? It seems we have nothing to offer, and can only receive what God offers to us in Christ for our salvation. I am convinced that Donald Baillie is correct when he asserts that we offer *ourselves* afresh in the celebration of the Lord's Supper. He draws an observation from the Orthodox tradition of bringing the bread and wine as an offering and laying it on the altar. He observes:

> That practice must have helped the faithful to feel that they were bringing the common life into God's presence, with its common tasks of ploughing and sowing and reaping and threshing and baking and all the other work that went into the making of bread.[26]

So we offer our work, leisure, powers, possessions and lives to God (cf. Romans 12:1-2 and Ephesians 2:8-10). The practice of the Harvest Thanksgiving at All Hallows by the Tower amongst London's finance and business community is a good example of this offering of everyday lives. Their service begins with the presentation of symbols, as the priest says:

We have come together to worship God, who is present with us in all that we do. In thanksgiving we each offer Him our daily lives, and especially in this place, our work.

The congregation remain standing while representatives from the Business Community bring to the altar symbols of the harvest of their working life, saying:
These offerings are presented to God as our thanksgiving for His creative presence in our lives and work

Once the symbols are presented, all say:
Yours, Lord, is the greatness, the power, the glory, the splendour, and the majesty; for everything in heaven and earth is yours. All things come from you, and of your own do we give you.

Amongst the symbols placed on the altar one year were: sweets and *petit fours* brought by a hotel; a model of the US Space Shuttle Discovery brought by a company that worked for the space industry; a bag of sugar brought by a representative of Tate & Lyle; and canvas money bags brought by a finance company.

(d) Discerning the body of Christ

Just before their church anniversary in 1994, the congregation of El Cordero de Dios Baptist Church in San Salvador decided that they would produce a new mural to hang at the front of the church, behind the communion table. They met together one evening and looked at a series of slides, which showed scenes of the church's life during the previous couple of years. Then each member drew pictures to represent something of that pilgrimage. After a little while they came back together and placed all the pictures on the floor and discussed them. They chose images that the group felt best represented their life as a church.

The resulting picture was sketched on a large plastic sheet (about 2 x 4 metres) and painted by the whole group; it was almost dawn when the mural was completed. The result is a striking banner of images that the whole church can appreciate and recognize as their own story. The images included scenes from the urban and rural communities that surrounded the church, the work activities of church members, and depictions of home life and worship. The people tell their own story in their art and they identify the Gospel story with their own story. Each time they celebrate the Lord's Supper their story is framed by the bread and wine.

We share bread and wine, but we recognize that our celebration is marred by lack of understanding and response. We notice that many of the problems and divisions at Corinth came into sharp focus at the Supper. Paul says, 'Here is my message to you. I have this to say about your celebration of the Supper—it isn't! It's not the Lord's Supper that you celebrate—your behaviour denies what you say you are doing' (1 Corinthians 11:20). How could such a situation be the Lord's Supper, when each person was only concerned with satisfying themselves—be it with food (1 Cor. 11:21-2), or divisive theological debate (1 Cor. 1:12-17), or through a competitive exercise of spiritual gifts (1 Cor. 12)? Paul had to insist that 'You are not discerning the broken body of Christ, the church'. They were failing to give attention to each other.

We cannot involve ourselves in violence, inequality, oppression, and immoral behaviour and then share one loaf and one cup; we cannot exploit God's creation and live in broken relationships with other people, and then enter into the death and resurrection of Christ. This is no mere memorial meal. Breaking and sharing one loaf, drinking from one cup, serves to emphasize the unity of one body—fellowship in and through Christ. Through the celebration of the supper, there is participation in the new covenant, through the death of Christ. The covenant community is established in this meal, a community demonstrating cross-shaped love and resurrection power. Bonhoeffer is right to stress the impossibility of Christian community without *agape*. He says: 'Human love breeds hothouse flowers; spiritual love creates the *fruits* that grow healthily in accord with God's good will in the rain and the storm and sunshine of God's outdoors.'[27]

The Lord's Supper is one place where we experience the presence of the Spirit, through whom we understand the action of Jesus and the love of the Father. This is an encounter with the triune God, the God of relationship. It therefore cannot be a private act, but an experience of the church, as together we are caught up into the relationship of God. We meet, then, two dimensions of holism in the Supper: a holism in the spirituality of the individual and a holism of the community as the body of Christ, or the priesthood of all believers. Anne Primavesi and Jennifer Henderson conclude that:

> In the practice of table companionship the harmony and reconciliation between the companions determines the Eucharist. If there is no care for one another, then the Lord's Supper is not celebrated. The bread is broken for judgement and not for blessing.[28]

This is the thrust of Paul's challenge to the Corinthian church in 1 Corinthians 11. But Howard Marshall notes that while the New Testament itself recognizes the difficulties that arise when the Lord's Supper is part of a common church meal, 'nevertheless, the linking of the Supper with a meal may offer a form of fellowship that could contribute to the edification of the church today.'[29]

The late David Watson suggests that the breakthrough to genuine fellowship comes when Christians stop trying to relate to each other as righteous saints and recognize the truth that we are all unrighteous sinners.[30] He observes that the eucharist is the clearest expression of Christian community (cf. Ephesians 2:13ff), where we look to God and say 'Father' and turn in love to each other and say 'my sister', 'my brother'. For it is here that we remember the measureless and matchless grace of God, and acknowledge our own sin. The Lord's Supper is a meal for sinners.[31]

Through our worship we express what it means to be the people of God. In our baptism we identify with Jesus and participate in his death and resurrection as a once-for-all act. As we celebrate the Lord's Supper, we re-enact the Gospel story, we hear the invitation of Jesus, we eat bread and drink wine and participate afresh in his death and resurrection. The Lord's Supper is embodied worship, a place to give attention to others. It is an encounter with Christ and an encounter with each other.

(e) Including all in the Supper

When we share bread and wine we give thanks for God's love for the whole world in Christ (John 3:16-17; 6:51). In Jesus' ministry we see that God's love is inclusive. When we look at the people whom Jesus met with and ate with we recognize that normal 'religious' codes of conduct have to be reassessed. Jesus upset the religious folk by the table fellowship he practised. 'This man welcomes sinners and eats with them!' (Luke 15:2) Jesus demonstrated the indiscriminate love of God. The disciples did not understand his relating to the Samaritan woman at the well (John 4:5-26); Simon the Pharisee did not approve of his relations with the woman at his house (Luke 7:36-50); God needed to break down Peter's inhibitions of eating with Cornelius (Acts 10), and for the Great Banquet they went out to the highways and byways to bring in the outcasts and strangers (Luke 14:15-24). God has no favourites, but we ourselves find security in boundaries, barriers, rules and regulations. Anne Primavesi and Jennifer Henderson rightly suggest that 'the ability to recognize and witness to the indiscriminate love of God in Jesus' table companionship with sinners is still the gift of the . . . Spirit.'[32] They believe that our Eucharistic celebration should mirror that of the early church in being based on the joy, bounty and inclusivity of all the meals that Jesus celebrated. They note that

> For the Oriental, table fellowship is a fellowship of life. Therefore the acceptance of the outcasts into table fellowship with Jesus would immediately be understood as an offer of salvation to guilty sinners and as an assurance of forgiveness.[33]

No wonder the religious leaders cry with horror, 'this man receives sinners and eats with them!' But it is here that we find the challenge to recognize the inclusiveness of God's offer of love and hospitality.

It is certainly true that Jesus shared table fellowship with a variety of people, as expressed in one of the Eucharistic liturgies from the Iona Community:

He was always the guest
In the homes of Peter and Jairus,
Martha and Mary, Joanna and Susanna,
he was always the guest.

At the meal tables of the wealthy
where he pled the case of the poor,
he was always the guest.

Upsetting polite company,
befriending isolated people,
welcoming the stranger,
he was always the guest.

But here,
at this table,
he is the host.

Those who wish to serve him
must first be served by him,
those who want to follow him
must first be fed by him,
those who would wash his feet
must first let him make them clean.[34]

At the table we are called to join with Christ's mission of drawing people into the freedom of forgiven life. But if, as Smith and Taussig suggest, the meal for early Christian communities functioned as a boundary marker, defining the special identity of the group, it is no wonder that eating with outcasts and with Gentiles produced tensions both inside and outside the group (see, for example, Mark 2:13-17 and Galatians 2:11-14).[35]

3. Attention to the body of Christ in the church meeting

It is important to consider the relationship between the celebration of the Lord's Supper and our understanding of what it means to be the local church of Christ. Paul Fiddes believes that the church meeting is sacramental, a conviction rooted in the continual gift of grace in creation. He says:

> The invitation into the body of Christ received in baptism is continued in the Lord's Supper and church meeting. . . . Immersion into the death and resurrection of Christ in baptism is to be renewed in eucharistic celebration and in corporate decision making about community lifestyle and service in the world.[36]

With Fiddes, I believe that the church, meeting together, enters into the mission of the trinitarian God. Elsewhere I have described the church meeting in trinitarian terms as: the children of the *Father*, meeting in the presence of the *Spirit*, to seek the mind of *Christ*.[37]

For Roman Catholics the Mass is an expression of spiritual unity, and those participate in it who are united in the church. There is a parallel in the fencing of the table and discipline found in early Baptist congregations. For Baptists, gathering at the table and in church meetings expresses our covenant together and with God. This is indicated by the early Baptist practice of holding a church meeting immediately following the celebration of the Lord's Supper, the minute books and membership roll being kept in a drawer of the communion table, or near to it.

We catch a glimpse of early Baptist covenanted communities through a picture of a typical Lord's Day amongst a seventeenth-century Baptist community at Kilmington and Loughwood in Devon. A meeting dated 31st of the 2nd Month, 1657 gave the following detailed timetable of services during the summer:

> 1. That the first day's meetings be begun (as near as may be) aboute seaven in the Morninge, and soe continue for the summer season. And the tyme employed as followeth. Vizt.

1. In the tryall of gifts till 9 of the clocke. And that those 2 howers be improved by way of prayer.

2. from 9 in the morninge till well towards 12 in a publique exercise.

3. from one till 3 of the clocke in publique exercise.

4. that after the demission of those that are nott members the church spend one hower or 2 in Communicatinge their experiences; inquiringe after persons absent; trying the things heard and dutys neglected.

2.That the next first day seavennight the church Breake Bread.[38]

John Whiteley, who has written the history of this church, is right to observe that this timetable gave a full day's activities, and that spending most of the daylight hours at Loughwood must have created a sense of community. Five hours of public worship and preaching ('exercise'), we notice, are followed by a two hour church meeting, and at least every two weeks the schedule included the Lord's Supper.

There is a unity between the celebration of the Lord's Supper and the church meeting. The celebration of sharing the bread and the wine gives the 'energy' for discipleship, and Christ's body broken for us constrains us to be that body broken for the world. Church members can encounter Christ in a 'bodily' way through the bread and wine and also through each other. Like the Lord's Supper the church meeting has individual and communal dimensions, since it is a place where individual opinions and beliefs may be expressed, but where together we seek God's will for his church. It is a place for waiting on God and for reaching a God-guided consensus.

We might consider, then, *how* decisions are reached in the church meeting. There are four help-lines that a church might call upon: scripture, prophecy, spiritual leadership and the wider church. It is the authority of Christ as revealed in scripture that directs the church, and it is scripture that will test the other sources of guidance. However, sin will show up in arguments; power struggles, envy and jealousy will sadly exist. We might think that all has been prayerfully agreed and that the conclusion has been reached through the mediation of the Spirit—the 'bond of peace' being preserved—when the reality has been altogether different. We might presume that everyone is in agreement, when actually people have not had a chance to voice their unhappiness with the decision. Some may feel that the church meeting is merely there to agree what 'they' have already decided. There may be a feeling that there is something behind the discussion which is not being openly stated, and people may leave the meeting unhappy that they do not apparently know the full story. An item may be left 'on the table', undecided, leaving members unhappy that they have not had an opportunity to discuss it. On the other hand, something may be pushed through very quickly, leaving people with the feeling that the issue has been rushed through without proper thought. Sometimes a proposal will be worded in such a way that it can only lead to one result, leaving people with the suspicion that it was rigged.[39]

Leaders should therefore ask themselves a number of questions. 'What are we doing to help every member of the group to speak the truth in love?' 'What are we doing to promote real understanding of the issues?' 'How are we listening for the voice of the Spirit?'[40]

I believe that we should always aim at consensus, for everyone matters and anyone may be the channel of God's direction for the church. When consensus is reached it includes all views from full agreement to 'I can live with this decision and I will not seek to undermine it.' Consensus takes far longer than 'like it or lump it,' and involves hearing everyone, not just the articulate, the confident or the domineering. Therefore there may be real benefit through breaking into smaller groups, which allow more people to speak. They will generally be more ready to express what they think in a small group. It is often helpful to use a flip-chart, where important points can be noted, and everyone can see the range of opinions and the general flow of the discussion. We look for consensus rather than majority opinion, since we have come prayerfully together, to know the mind of Christ. Nevertheless, we must always be ready to hear God speaking through the least expected voice in the meeting. The church meeting expresses the Baptist spirituality of holding together both individual liberty and the discipline of the community.[41] The church meeting is the place where the congregation explores its place and role in the mission of Christ in the world. When people speak we trust that we hear the individual *prophet*; but when the church comes to a decision, it is to act as the corporate *priest*.

Like the members, the pastor too has an individual role. Alan Roxburgh observes that pastors in the later twentieth century became characterized as teachers, counsellors, and professionals, but that these descriptors have ceased to be meaningful at the beginning of the twenty-first century. However, because the paradigm is so entrenched, 'practically the only model presented to each new generation of potential leaders is pastor as professional and teacher; the caretaker and chaplain of dwindling, ageing congregations.'[42] Young creative leaders, with the passion and skills desperately needed in the churches, see this model and turn elsewhere for vocational fulfilment.

In a time of declining congregations Roxburgh notes that there is a need for leaders who listen to the voices from the edge. 'This is where the *apostle*, the *poet*, and the *prophet* are found. These are the metaphors for congregational leadership today.'[43] These are different leaders, who are encountered by, and in turn encounter, our culture with the gospel. The apostle holds out the gospel story in stark contrast to the cultural context, leading churches into a missionary encounter and equipping disciples. The poet is an articulator of experience, who images and symbolizes the unarticulated experiences of the community, identifying and expressing the soul of the people within their culture. The prophet addresses the word of God directly into the experience of the people of God, and offers a vision of God's purposes for them in the transformation of culture. All these roles, however, are to be performed in the context of the whole church as the 'royal priesthood' of Christ.

4. Christ's mission in and for the world

The celebration of the Lord's Supper brings our Sunday and Monday worlds together. It is thanksgiving to God for everything that God has accomplished in creation, redemption and sanctification, and for God's work of bringing the kingdom to fulfilment in spite of human sin. As William Lazareth states:

> The very celebration of the Eucharist is an instance of the Church's participation in God's mission to the world. This participation takes everyday form in the proclamation of the Gospel, service of neighbour and faithful presence in the world.[44]

The incarnation in history demonstrates God's clear identification with the created world of space and time. The celebration of the Lord's Supper with its backward look to the life, death and resurrection of Christ, and its forward look to the hope of the consummation of the world in God's eternal kingdom, celebrated in the physical elements of bread and wine, embraces the whole of life and human existence. Lazareth rightly concludes that:

> Solidarity in the Eucharistic communion of the body of Christ and responsible care of Christians for one another and the world find specific expression in the liturgies: in mutual forgiveness of sins; the sign of peace; intercession for all; the eating and drinking together; the taking of the elements to the sick and those in prison or the celebration of the Eucharist with them.[45]

This is the love and ministry of the servant Christ in which we share and in whose mission we participate.

In an interesting collection of essays Michael Ramsey and Cardinal Suenens discuss the future of the church.[46] Ramsey believes that the church is here to serve the world through challenging the world's assumptions and demonstrating that the world's greatest need is to humbly recognize its need of God's love and desire for human living. He states that 'the sacrament of the body and blood of Christ in the Eucharist belongs to the timeless participation of Christians in his death and resurrection. There the church renews its faith in the God who is true and living.'[47] Suenens moves us on in our understanding through his belief that to understand the relationship between the church and the world we should first examine the relationship between *Christ* and the world, as the church is to be seen as the 'sacramental presence of Christ.'[48]

A challenging illustration of such a presence is found in the words of the 'Misa Campesina', the 'Peasant Mass' which emerged from the community founded in the 1960s by Ernesto Cardenal on the island of Solentiname in Lake Nicaragua. Andrew Bradstock and Christopher Rowland state that 'it attempts to "demystify" the Christ of more conventional liturgies, and portray him, without stooping to irreverence, as one of the people, a *companero* in the struggle to forge the new society.'[49] The following is an indicative selection:

You are the God of the poor
the human and simple God
the God that sweats in the street
the God with the weathered face
that is why I speak to you
like my people speak
because you are the labourer God
the worker Christ.

Hand in hand you walk with my people
you struggle in the fields and the city
you stand in line at the camp
in order to be paid your day's wages . . .

I firmly believe, Lord
that from your fertile thought
this whole world was born;
that from your artist's hand,
like a primativist painter,
all beauty flourished . . .

I believe in you
architect, engineer,
artisan, carpenter,
bricklayer and shipbuilder . . .

I believe in you, Companero
human Christ, worker Christ
conqueror of death
by your immense sacrifice
you have begotten the new human
who is destined for liberation.
You are alive in every arm
that raises itself to defend the people
because you are alive in the ranch
in the factory, in the school
I believe in your struggle without truce
I believe in your resurrection.

Suenens helpfully maintains that the church should communicate three aspects of Christ's relationship with the world:

- That Christ is *in and for* the world in creation, the realm of the natural world, and through the incarnation.
- That Christ is *against* the world, standing against the forces of destruction and alienation, and exposing the ambiguity of sin.
- That Christ is *beyond* the world in redeeming death, through life-giving revelation, and as the world's eternal hope.

In similar vein Lesslie Newbigin maintains that the Last Supper Discourse (John 13-16) and the prayer of Jesus (John 17) are an exposition of the meaning of the Supper.[50] Here in this discourse the way of discipleship is sketched out, as the first disciples, and we in our time, represent Jesus in the world. Key themes develop in Jesus' discourse, arising from the very action of the Supper: servanthood, abiding in Christ, knowing the way in Christ, receiving the gift of the Spirit, producing fruit through abiding in Christ, experiencing hatred in the world, understanding the Spirit's conviction of the world in rebellion against God, and the Spirit's guidance into truth. Jesus' prayer was for the continuance of his mission in the same power of consecration that he received from God

(John 17:20-26). Paul Fiddes expresses this thought when he suggests that:

> as the members of the church share in bread and wine, Christ takes hold more firmly of their own bodies and uses them as a means of his presence in the world. Just as Christ uses the physical stuff of bread and wine as a meeting-place between himself and his disciples, so he uses their bodies as a means of encountering them through each other, and as a meeting-place with those outside the church.

So, Fiddes concludes, 'the church itself becomes a sacrament, and participates bodily in the mission of God in the world. In some sense . . . it also becomes an extension of the incarnation.'[51] We can therefore stress that the dismissal at the end of the liturgy is a going out into the world, a participating in the Father's sending of the Son (John 20:21-22). This truth is conveyed in the notice on the *inside* (only readable on leaving) of many Baptist church doors: 'You are now entering God's mission field.' Fiddes develops this thought by affirming that mission takes the form of community; the church 'goes out' by opening up its life to draw in the alien, the outcast and the stranger just as God makes room for us in God's own life of communion. He suggests that

> The most effective form of mission may be the impact of the community life of the church on its neighbourhood, not enclosed in self-preservation but open in risky welcome. Mission will thus be concerned with making relations at every level of the world, in reflection of the triune God.[52]

We are one in Christ, together and individually; the bread is broken and the cup shared, and taken into individual bodies. We share the one loaf and the gathering church becomes the scattered church—taking Christ out into the world, where in our different places we all together make up the body of Christ and a priesthood; we are Christ to and for the world.

At the table we are called to join Christ in his mission in and for the world. We are sharing the gospel imperative of drawing people into the freedom of forgiven and renewed life. We declare our faith in Christ as we come to the table, and here we offer an open invitation to others. Eleanor Kreider reminds us of John Wesley's observation of 'the converting power of the Eucharist.' It is here that God issues his invitation afresh: 'Come to me all you who are weary and burdened, and I will give you rest' (Matthew 11:28). Kreider notes that if it is the Lord's Supper then it is the Lord and not the church that issues the invitation. So, she maintains, it is not the place for human discipline—the church's evaluation of a person's standing—for no one, but Christ, is worthy. She concludes, 'The Lord's table is spread for a feast of joy, not a worrisome lament.'[53] We are invited to share in Christ's self-giving ministry.

I believe that the development over the last twenty years of the *Alpha* programme for evangelism gives some important pointers toward mission and discipleship focused in the celebration of the Lord's Supper. The principle aims of *Alpha* are to present the gospel in a non-threatening environment, where participants can discuss the claims of Christianity; this means, usually, over a meal in someone's home. As a response to those who consider *Alpha* to be entirely separate from Sunday worship we listen to Eleanor Kreider's question: 'Isn't it possible that a way to renewal of Sunday Eucharistic worship could be through reclaiming Jesus' own approach of love for outsiders, his radical invitations, and his generous table hospitality?'[54] She notes that Jesus ate meals with his disciples and with outcasts and sinners, and that we should regard both forms of hospitality as messianic feasts, and as visions of the Great Banquet of heaven.

This is our participation in the mission of God, who is on a journey into the world to seek the lost. Anne Primavesi and Jennifer Henderson stress that 'Those who live with open hands belong to the kingdom. Through the power of the Spirit they remember the death and resurrection of Jesus and the openness of his self-giving whenever bread is broken and wine is shared among them'.[55] This becomes the fundamental basis for mission.

This mission, moreover, cannot be confined to the human community. We recognize that the Lord's Supper extends beyond the church congregation to the whole world. We understand God to be present in all human life, and beyond this to his work in sustaining the whole environment. We understand that God is immanent in the whole of creation, and that in the incarnation he declares his solidarity with the whole of the created order. We recognize that redemption and restoration of the poor, weak and vulnerable includes the atmosphere, biosphere and ecosystems of the world we inhabit.

Sallie McFague, in her essay on *An Ecological Christology*,[56] urges the church to answer the question 'How have you been committed to the reign of God?' She believes that the natural world might be envisaged as 'the new poor,' believing that justice, rights, care and concern should be extended to the whole of creation. She challenges us to recognize that Jesus' ministry to God's oppressed creatures must include our deteriorating planet. For McFague, sacramental Christology is the embodiment of God in creation, as well as the hope of new creation.

Sean McDonagh suggests that we explore the Eucharist as renewing the covenant.[57] He focuses on two themes: covenant renewal, and thanksgiving to God for all gifts including the gift of creation. Covenant living includes praise and thanksgiving, and care of the poor and of the vulnerable. The new covenant in Christ includes the political freedom and promised land of the old covenant but, in addition, is the inauguration of the kingdom of God. God's work in creation is in the background of all the covenants, especially the covenant with Noah. Sadly, our misuse, overuse, and abuse are 'shredding the integrity of creation.'[58] To be covenant people we need to learn to understand and work in harmony with creation. This requires humility. McDonagh suggests that on a number of occasions each year our celebration of the Eucharist should highlight the renewal of the cosmic covenant where the emphasis would be on promoting work for justice and the integrity of creation among Christians.[59]

Thanksgiving has also been a central focus of the Eucharist, from Passover remembrance to our recalling the love of God in Christ. McDonagh notes that the Jewish *berakah* (prayer of blessing and thanks) from which all eucharistic prayers are ultimately derived, gave thanks first for God's natural bounty and secondly for the blessings of the covenant.[60] The dynamic creation of which we are a part should be reflected in our eucharistic celebration, and could include our appreciation of our own local environment. Such prayers, urges McDonagh, would reconnect a worshipping people with their immediate landscape, and thence their lives with the whole of creation.[61]

He concludes that the eucharistic gifts of bread and wine symbolize the gifts of creation and the human dimension of care and creativity in fashioning these elements into food and drink. Here is the mutual relationship between individual human beings, the social world of dependence on others, and the natural world. We are challenged to an ethical lifestyle and celebrate the Holy Spirit renewing us and the whole of creation.[62]

5. Conclusion

I began by proposing a wide definition of what it means to be spiritual—to seek to live in the presence of God and to be involved with the things of God. We might interpret 'spiritual' in New Testament terms through the concept of personal, that is, through the understanding of relationships, where true relationships are personal relationships. It is our personal relationship with God, expressed through our worship, and focused in the celebration of the Lord's Supper, that is the basis of our spirituality. To repeat the words of William Stringfellow in *The Politics of Spirituality*, spirituality 'involves the whole person . . . in connection with the whole of creation throughout the era of time.'[63]

The sharing of bread and wine is the focus for the realization of our relationship with God, with each other, and with the world which God has created. The sense of participation that we have been emphasizing is not only significant for the way in which we understand and celebrate the Lord's Supper (and baptism), it is also significant for our understanding of what it means to be church. It concerns not only our personal spirituality and relationship with God, but also our corporate spirituality as the 'body of Christ.' It is in our gathering at the Table, where we remember the death and resurrection of Christ that we become who we are—the true body of Christ in and for the world.

We come together to be the body of Christ (1 Peter 2:4-5, 9) and retell the story of God's loving sacrifice for us in Christ. We recognize that the table fellowship, the celebration of the Lord's Supper, and the recounted story are truly sacramental in demonstrating a community of God's people expressing love and forgiveness through their shared lives. Through the celebration of the Supper the community of the church becomes the body of Christ broken for the life of the world.

In the Supper we participate in the death and resurrection of Christ, dying to self and rising to new life in the power of the Spirit, and we discover forgiveness and restoration, renewed to be Christ for the world. It is here in the one loaf shared that the gathering community becomes the priesthood of believers (the one priest, Christ), and in the one loaf broken that the community scattered becomes the priesthood of believers (the one priest, Christ) in service in and for the world.

Here is just one symbol of that reality. The churches together in Rushden, Northamptonshire hold a united outreach on Good Friday each year in the middle of the (pedestrianized) High Street. One year following a dramatic presentation of the crucifixion each of the town's clergy took a large freshly baked loaf, which had been lying at the foot of the cross. They took these and broke them and offered the broken pieces to all who had gathered.

There is, I believe, a particular Baptist contribution to this theme in the interaction between the Lord's Supper and the church meeting. There is an element of the individual and the corporate in both; in Supper and meeting we individually covenant with God, finding forgiveness and salvation, and yet also covenant with each other in seeking the ministry and mission of Christ. Both the Lord's Supper and the church meeting are expressions of the 'body of Christ.' The Supper and the meeting both have a present reality of being the body of Christ and an eschatological focus in the consummation of the kingdom of God. In the Supper the community comes together to seek the presence of Christ in a deeper way, and in the church meeting it comes together to seek the mind of Christ, in a desire to share in his mission in and for the world. In all of this we aim to follow in the footsteps of our Baptist forebears who sought to 'walk together and watch over each other in love.'

Notes

[1] See Paul in Romans 6:1-11.

[2] William Stringfellow, *The Politics of Spirituality* (Philadelphia: Westminster Press, 1984) p. 22, quoted in Alister McGrath, *Christian Spirituality. An Introduction* (Oxford: Blackwell, 1999), p. 4.

[3] Paul S. Fiddes, *Participating in God: A Pastoral Doctrine of the Trinity* (London: Darton, Longman and Todd, 2000), pp. 89, 281.

[4] John M Hull, *What Prevents Adults from Learning?* (Philadelphia: Trinity Press International, 1991) p. 7.

[5] John 2:1-11.

[6] Paul S Fiddes, 'Baptism and Creation' in Paul S. Fiddes (ed.), *Reflections on the Water. Understanding God and the World through the Baptism of Believers* (Macon: Smyth & Helwys/ Oxford: Regent's Park College, 1996), p. 63.

[7] Dennis E. Smith and Hal E. Taussig, *Many Tables. The Eucharist in the New Testament and Liturgy Today* (London: SCM Press/ Philadelphia: Trinity Press International, 1990), pp. 31-4.

[8] Eleanor Kreider, *Communion Shapes Character* (Scottdale: Herald Press, 1997), p.242. Also published in UK as *Given for You: a Fresh Look at Communion* (Leicester: Apollos/IVP, 1998) although page numbers will vary.

[9] Keith Jones, *A Believing Church. Learning from some Contemporary Anabaptist and Baptist Perspectives* (Didcot: Baptist Union of Great Britain, 1998), p. 12.

[10] Jones, *A Believing Church*, p. 44.

[11] James William McClendon Jnr, *Systematic Theology*. Volumes 1 & 2 (Nashville: Abingdon Press, 1986, 1994), quoted in Jones, *A Believing Church*, p. 52.

[12] http://www.reformed.org/documents/index.html?mainframe=http://www.reformed.org/documents/westminster_conf_of_faith.html, accessed 30.03.06.

[13] *Confession of Faith Put Forth by the Elders and Brethren Of many Congregations Of Christians (baptized upon Profession of their Faith)* (London: 1677), XXX, in W.L. Lumpkin, *Baptist Confessions of Faith* (Chicago: Judson Press, 1959), p. 293.

[14] See argument developed by Eleanor Kreider, *Communion Shapes Character*, pp. 114-18.

[15] Kreider, *Community Shapes Character*, p. 153.

[16] Smith & Taussig, *Many Tables*, p. 80.

[17] Donald M. Baillie, *The Theology of the Sacraments* (London: Faber & Faber, 1957), p. 101.

[18] Thomas H. Groome, *Christian Religious Education: Sharing our Story and Vision* (San Francisco: Harper & Row, 1980), p. 193.

[19] C. F. D. Moule, *The Sacrifice of Christ* (London: Hodder & Stoughton, 1956), pp. 32-3.

[20] I have described these stories in more detail in: John Weaver, *Outside-In. Theological Reflection on Life* (Macon: Smyth & Helwys/ Oxford: Regent's Park College, 2006), pp. 30-1.

[21] Paul S. Fiddes, *Tracks and Traces. Baptist Identity in Church and Theology.* (Carlisle: Paternoster, 2003), p. 169.

[22] Kreider, *Communion Shapes Character*, p. 242.

[23] John W. de Gruchy, *Reconciliation. Restoring Justice* (London: SCM, 2002), p. 96.

[24] Fiddes, *Participating in God*, p. 281.

[25] Fiddes, *Tracks and Traces,* p. 168.

[26] Baillie, *Theology of the Sacraments*, p. 115.

[27] Dietrich Bonhoeffer, *Life Together* (London: SCM Press, 1954), p. 24.

[28] Anne Primavesi and Jennifer Henderson, *Our God has no Favorites. A Liberation Theology of the Eucharist* (Tunbridge Wells: Burns & Oates, 1989), p. 92.

[29] I. Howard Marshall, *Last Supper and Lord's Supper* (Exeter: Paternoster, 1980), p. 157.

[30] David Watson, *Discipleship* (London: Hodder & Stoughton, 1981), p. 52.

[31] Watson, *Discipleship*, p. 62.

[32] Primavesi & Henderson, *Our God has no Favorites,* p. 34.

[33] Primavesi & Henderson, *Our God has no Favorites*, p. 41.

[34] John L. Bell and Mairi Munro, Wild Goose Worship Group, *A Wee Worship Book* (Glasgow: Wild Goose Publications, 1999), p. 84, used with kind permission of the publishers.

[35] Smith & Taussig, *Many Tables*, pp. 59-60.

[36] Fiddes, 'Baptism and Creation', p. 64.

[37] John Weaver, 'The Church Meeting' in Derek Tidball, *Baptist Basics* (Didcot: Baptist Union of Great Britain, 1993).

[38] John Whiteley, 'The Early History. Life at Loughwood' in *From Backwoods to Beacon. Kilmington Baptist Church, the first 350 years* (Kilmington Baptist Church, 2000). Available in The Angus Library, Regent's Park College, Oxford.

[39] Based on Colin Patterson, *How to Learn through Conflict. A Handbook for Leaders in Local Churches*. Grove Pastoral Series (Cambridge: Grove Books, 2003).

[40] Patterson, *How to Learn through Conflict*.

[41] This tension between individual and community was explored in the previous chapter, by James Gordon.

[42] Alan Roxburgh, 'Pastoral Role in the Missionary Congregation' in G. Hunsberger and C. Van Gelder (eds), *Church Between Gospel and Culture* (Grand Rapids: Eerdmans, 1996), p. 321.

[43] Roxburgh, 'Pastoral Role in the Missionary Congregation', pp. 325-6.

[44] William H Lazareth, *Growing Together in Baptism, Eucharist and Ministry. A Study Guide* (Geneva: WCC, 1983), p. 51.

[45] Lazareth, *Growing Together in Baptism, Eucharist and Ministry*, p. 73.

[46] A. M. Ramsey and L.-J. Suenens, *The Future of the Christian Church* (London: SCM Press, 1970).

[47] Ramsey & Suenens, *The Future of the Christian Church*, p. 28.

[48] Ramsey & Suenens, *The Future of the Christian Church*, p. 64.

[49] Sylvia Mullally and Tony Ryan, 'Misa Campesina' in *Nicaraguan Perspectives*; translation by Mullally and Ryan based on *Misa Campesina Nicaragüense*, published by the Ministry of Culture, Managua, Nicaragua, 1981, quoted in Andrew Bradstock & Christopher Rowland (eds), *Radical Christian Writings. A Reader* (Oxford: Blackwell, 2002), pp. 243-6.

[50] Lesslie Newbigin, *The Open Secret. An Introduction to the Theology of Mission* (London: SPCK, 1995), pp. 46-7.

[51] Fiddes, *Tracks and Traces*, p. 170.

[52] Fiddes, *Tracks and Traces*, p. 254.

[53] Kreider, *Communion shapes Character*, p. 251.

[54] Kreider, *Communion shapes Character*, p. 253.

[55] Primavesi & Henderson, *Our God has no Favorites*, p. 7.

[56] Sallie McFague, 'An Ecological Christology. Does Christianity have it?' in Richard C. Foltz (ed.), *Worldviews, Religion, and the Environment. A Global Anthology* (Belmont: California / Wadsworth: Thomson Learning, 2003), pp. 336-8.

[57] Sean McDonagh, *Greening the Christian Millennium* (Dublin: Dominican Publications, 1999), pp. 193-213.

[58] McDonagh, *Greening the Christian Millennium,* p. 197.

[59] McDonagh, *Greening the Christian Millennium,* p. 201.

[60] McDonagh, *Greening the Christian Millennium,* p. 203.

[61] See, for example, my own meditation, printed as the postscript in *Earthshaping Earthkeeping* (London: SPCK/Lynx, 1999).

[62] McDonagh, *Greening the Christian Millennium,* p. 213.

[63] Stringfellow, *Politics of Spirituality*, p. 4.

7
Spirituality in Mission: Gathering and Grace

Christopher Ellis

Certain words have a particular potency for particular groups. These words seem to sum up the identity which holds them together, the values which select priorities and the vision which leads people forward. These words energize, motivate and call people back to basics. 'Mission' is such a word for Baptists and much will be attempted if 'mission' is the rallying cry. Ecumenical friends acknowledge that in local ecumenism Baptist patience for structural discussions may be strictly limited, but 'mission' will mobilize where unity schemes do not.

Such missionary concerns have both local and international dimensions. In the early twentieth century Henry Wheeler Robinson commented, 'It is in the missionary meeting that you may hear the beating of the Baptist heart.'[1] Robinson was probably referring to an institutional meeting to support 'overseas' missionary work but this reference illustrates and supports a missionary attitude which he regarded as typical of much Baptist church life for it appears in a chapter entitled 'The Missionary Spirit of the Baptists'. Indeed, we can observe that the third article of the Declaration of Principle of the Baptist Union of Great Britain reminds us, 'That it is the duty of every disciple to bear personal witness to the Gospel of Jesus Christ, and to take part in the evangelization of the world'. 'Remind' is probably the right verb, as the declaration is an instrument of unity and as such must use means which are attractive to those being united. Internationally, Baptists continue to offer this missionary profile. The second objective of the Baptist World Alliance is, 'To bear witness to the gospel of Jesus Christ and assist member bodies in their divine task of bringing all people to God through Jesus Christ as Saviour and Lord.'[2]

Two questions immediately come to the fore. First, is this rhetoric a true representation of Baptist priorities and, if so, is it integral to the life and concerns of individuals as well as churches and organizations?

Secondly, has it always been so, such that Baptists can claim to possess a missionary gene which marks and influences the denomination's DNA? The questions are, of course, related and can be reformulated into another, more penetrating inquiry: do these missionary concerns grow out of a Baptist ecclesial identity? The answer to each of these questions is in the affirmative, though not without caveat and qualification. As so often with matters of identity, we need to distinguish between what is *naturally* the case, flowing from who we are at our best—and what is *often* the case, beguiling us away from the integrity of our confessional vision.

But what has mission to do with spirituality? Provided we use a holistic definition of spirituality which is broader than simply the life of devotion, then the connections should become clear. Philip Sheldrake offers such a definition:

> Spirituality is understood to include not merely the techniques of prayer but, more broadly, a conscious relationship with God, in Jesus Christ, through the indwelling of the Spirit and in the context of the community of believers. Spirituality is, therefore, concerned with the conjunction of theology, prayer and practical Christianity.[3]

Theology, prayer and practical Christianity—this conjunction offers an inclusive vision of life before, with and in God. This life in the Spirit involves what we believe and what we do, as well as how we relate to God. The missionary heartbeat to which Wheeler Robinson referred is a heartbeat which circulates lifeblood between the head, the heart and the hands. In a very limited way this paper will ask how missionary concerns relate to theology, devotion and action within the British Baptist community. This, I believe, will explore the characteristics of Baptist spirituality which will also be found in other Baptist communities throughout the world. I shall briefly examine the story of the past and then reflect upon some ecclesial and theological connections within our denominational identity. Then, having identified a number of present day concerns I shall suggest two theological affirmations which might help us navigate some of the treacherous waters of contemporary culture.

1. Attention to Christ and the Great Commission: The missionary past

Baptists in Britain have never been a large group when compared to other mainstream denominations, though they have sometimes shown signs of vigour. Writing about the various churches in London at the beginning of the twentieth century, Charles Booth commented that the worship of the Baptists was very similar to that of the Congregationalists, but described Baptist life as 'virile' with an emphasis on doctrine and piety.[4] Similarly we may note that while Baptist churches have declined through that century in company with other denominations, that decline has in recent decades been slower than that of others.

Yet the story is complex. There were, of course various Baptist groups which in turn had varying approaches to mission. The General Baptists, for example, grew rapidly, although, after the early years, they never outnumbered the Particulars.[5] They had a strong emphasis on associating and their Arminian theology led them to place considerable emphasis on preaching the gospel. Factors which led to their demise by the end of the eighteenth century included a particular form of biblical literalism which, on the one hand, failed to resist the corrosive influence of Enlightenment categories in doctrine while, on the other hand, undergirded a very conservative approach to worship. For example, the rejection of congregational singing would have resulted in worship which would not have had a wide appeal in a culture where the Evangelical Revival in general, and Methodism in particular, was making headway with the general population. Hymn singing, while not a matter of doctrinal life and death, nonetheless remained at the centre of the growing separation between the old General Baptists and Dan Taylor and those who eventually formed the General Baptists of the New Connexion.[6]

For the Particular Baptists the story is sufficiently complex, especially in relation to the eighteenth century, for modern historians to debate the facts. The traditional interpretation of events—if the evolution of theology can be described as 'events'—has been that the Enlightenment impacted Particular Baptist life by encouraging the rationalistic extremes of Hyper Calvinism. John Gill is usually presented as the influential representative of this development and the hold of this theology has been seen as something which had to be broken before significant progress could be made in the area of mission. The Northamptonshire Association, with Fuller, Sutcliffe and Carey, has been seen as the place where this hold was eventually broken through the development of 'Fullerism', or modified Calvinism, the call to prayer for mission, Carey's emphasis that the Great Commission in Matthew 28 remained valid, and his exemplifying this vocation in his own life.

On the other hand, Roger Hayden has persuasively argued that too much attention has been paid to Gill and the London scene and that a strand of evangelical Calvinism can be identified running from the seventeenth century through the witness of the Bristol Academy and its principals, as well as the associations outside London. This Fullerism before Fuller is perhaps most clearly seen in the liturgical practice of preachers 'offering Christ' during worship—an evangelistic activity which was denounced by Hyper Calvinists.[7]

Either way, the establishing of a modern Protestant missionary society in 1792 was not only historically significant, the first of a number of such societies to be established in the next few decades, but it marked a new Baptist self-understanding as a missionary community. This overseas initiative was soon to be followed by national and local institutions concerned with missionary activity and a century of church planting and church building redevelopment. As with other free churches, British Baptists reached their statistical high water mark in the first decade of the twentieth century.[8] Since then there have been many calls to missionary activity and much Baptist church life has mirrored the concerns of other evangelical groups, and many churches have been keen to use the latest evangelistic programmes as they have appeared, often from North America. Decline brings its own pathology, and one feature to which we must pay particular attention when considering mission is the matter of motivation. Theology needs to undergird any church activity and mission is no exception, as Ian Stackhouse has so clearly demonstrated in his critique of Revivalism.[9] Fear of being a minority is a reasonable human response to a period of decline, but it will distort missionary endeavour if it is the dominant motive for evangelistic activity.

2. Attention to Christ the Lord of the church: ecclesial reflections

Any expedition into the world of ecclesiology and any reflection on the nature of denominational identity will need to distinguish between 'is' and 'ought', between the honesty of self-description and the challenge of normative and aspirational claims. The missionary clause of the *Declaration of Principle* is a good example of this dilemma: it may be a description of the stated values of churches which associate in the Union, but it is not a description of the practice of each member of each church. What does it mean to be 'a missionary people', as the first of the influential *5 Core Values for a Gospel People* expresses it?[10] This is not the place to enter a comprehensive debate of the pastoral, theological and spiritual issues implied in such a situation. Rather, we shall reflect on the ecclesiological perspectives of being a mission-shaped church and, in particular, those Baptist distinctives which interact to make the missionary imperative a core conviction of Baptist churches. To do so may seem like stating the obvious, but an audit of historical and contemporary concerns is an important contribution to any reflection on the values of the Christian community.

First, we may note the way in which Baptist origins are to be located in the desire to be a 'believer church'. Both General and Particular Baptists emerged from Separatist groups which, early in the seventeenth century, sought to return to what they believed to be the New Testament witness, namely, that the church is a body made up of believers. They rejected the notion of a state church and believed that the purity of the body of Christ was an obligation which had ecclesiological implications.

Second, it was from this believer church stance that their reading of the New Testament led to the conviction that only believers should be baptized.[11] Believing needed to precede belonging, and baptism was the ordinance which God provided which both marked the one baptized as an obedient disciple as well as a believer, and reminded the church of its origins in the gospel of Christ.

We shall return to both these themes, but we may note here that, third, discipleship has normally for Baptists been a significant model of being a Christian. Such a discipleship model can express well the perspective of a life lived in paying attention to Jesus Christ and a community of disciples offers an attentive and active model of church life. Perhaps something of our activist spirituality has flowed from this source, but following Jesus and being obedient to God's will are positive and life-affirming concerns. Ecclesiologically, we may note the historical interest in re-ordering the worship of the community on the basis of what were perceived to be divine commands,[12] and William Carey's argument for world mission rested on the similar foundation of what Jesus commanded his disciples to do. Here attention to scripture and attention to Christ were united in what was portrayed as a binding imperative. Discipleship and witness thus become closely related themes as any disciples worth their salt are going to attempt to obey this, the last command (according to Matthew) of the earthly Jesus. An important contemporary ecclesial expression of this obedience may be seen in the placing of mission at the heart of the agenda of a Baptist church meeting. If such a meeting is a demonstration of communal discipleship, as the community seeks to discern the mind of Christ and then find ways of implementing that mind in its life and witness, then we can see that discipleship and witness are closely wedded, both in individual and corporate expressions. Organizationally, this has sometimes resulted in vigorous programmes of church planting and, sometimes, a regular scrutiny of the life of the congregation as to whether its structures and its practices serve or hinder the mission of God.

Finally, we cannot leave the area of ecclesiology without acknowledging that attention to Christ as Lord of the church is not simply an important ecclesiastical strategy but a practice which enacts a truth at the very heart of the church. The Lordship of Christ is a dominant theme in Baptist reflections on the nature of the church, as the title of this book illustrates, and that living reality will find expression and be nurtured by the worship of the community as it gathers 'in the name of Jesus'. It is therefore reasonable to expect that Baptist worship will both express and nurture the missionary imperative. Reference has already been made to the offering of Christ by the preacher and the expectation that worship will be an arena in which God will engage with those on the threshold of faith is widespread. If the gospel of Christ is preached then the expectation that there will be a human response is quite reasonable, though the activity of the Spirit in that human response is sometimes ignored or subverted by human arrangements. But liturgical missionary focus should go far beyond evangelistic preaching. The whole of worship, in so far as it engages with God, is engaging with a missionary God, an incarnational God, a gracious God who invites and welcomes as well as sends. This divine missionary characteristic is most clearly seen in Jesus Christ and any worship which pays proper attention to Jesus will inevitably celebrate the transforming grace of God and turn its attention to the world for which Christ died.

There are a number of features of contemporary Baptist life which both display this missionary concern and also alert us to some dysfunctional possibilities. The conjunction—and interaction—of theology, prayer and practice is important for the health of each sphere as well as for the integrity and health of the whole. Mission practice, for example, needs constantly to be supported by prayer, just as it needs to be monitored and informed by theology.

This theological scrutiny will reflect the doctrinal confessions of the universal church, but it will also be helpful if those doctrines, in tackling questionable practices, engage with denominational culture and emphases. This is where history and denominational identity intersect with vision and continuing development. In what follows I wish to focus on two themes of spiritual theology which may be cut from the Baptist quarry and, with reshaping, be helpful to us in building healthy missionary activity in the future. These themes are the call to holy living and a firm grasp of the grace of God.

3. Spirituality and a mission for the whole of life

One of the tensions which has persisted through much of the Baptist story is the struggle between the life of the church and life in the world. Jürgen Moltmann has suggested that the church is called to live in the tension between two poles—relevance and identity (i.e. self-identity)—and that different circumstances will result in different responses to this challenge.[13] This is a constant dialectic where the temptation is often wholly to embrace one pole at the expense of the other. Yet both are required to ensure ecclesial health and faithfulness. If relevance becomes the dominant value, then the church's identity may be at risk which, in turn, will threaten its actual relevance. If identity is safeguarded at the cost of the church's relevance then even that identity is put at risk.

In the introductory chapter of his *A History of the English Baptists,* A.C. Underwood remarks that in the sociological categories of Ernst Troeltsch, Baptists 'belong unmistakably' to the sect-type rather than the church-type of Christian community.[14] They see themselves as 'a believer church' and as 'a gathered church'. Their origins are in the Reformation project of searching for a pure church and that purity has been sought through biblical exegesis, devotional challenge and church discipline. The restoring of what were perceived to be patterns of New Testament ecclesiology was accompanied by continual calls for sincerity and whole-hearted commitment. In turn, a strict approach to church discipline would see the transgressions of church members being sorrowfully discussed in a church meeting and often resulting in barring from the Lord's Table for a period. The First London Confession of 1644 declared that believers were to live under the rule of Christ, 'to live their lives in his walled sheepfold, and watered garden, to have communion here with the Saints, that they may be made partakers of their inheritance in the Kingdom of God'.[15]

In some ways, this may have been little different from the approach to discipline in some other traditions in the seventeenth and eighteenth centuries. However, what was fairly distinctive was the requirement that new members not only assent to the creed but give evidence of a personal faith and a changed life. When asked concerning the requirements for receiving someone into the church, the assembled representatives at the association meeting in Taunton in 1654 declared that it was not sufficient to assent to the creed and to church order but that there needed to be 'a declaration of an experimental work of the Spirit upon the heart . . . being attended with evident tokens of conversion . . .'.[16] This must have been a significant filter to a wholesale joining of Baptist churches. Yet a version has persisted in many churches up to the present, where church meetings receive reports on the testimony and readiness for church membership of prospective members. This is what Moltmann might mean by guarding the identity of the church.

Here is both pastoral and spiritual challenge as local churches navigate between the twin dangers of isolationist perfectionism and cultural accommodation. The tension cannot be resolved in this world as faithful living and faithful witness are both part of the calling of the messianic community.[17] However, there are two ways in which a contemporary response to this challenge may be resourced by engaging with the Baptist past. Both responses involve aspects of our broad understanding of spirituality.

First, we have noted Sheldrake's observation that spirituality is to be located within 'the context of the community of believers'. Baptists have traditionally understood the gathered nature of the *ekklesia* as a fundamental characteristic of the church which will result in its 'gathered' nature. Those who separated from the Church of England under Elizabeth and James were rejecting a Christendom model of church. Mission, therefore, would not only mean proclaiming the gospel of Christ, but gathering into this disciplined community those who appeared to show genuine signs of faith. Whether such an ecclesial community could ever be anything other than a minority church is not only a question of historical speculation but of missiological challenge. It invites exploration within the arena of Christian spirituality for it not only raises questions about what it means to be a Christian, as well as what it means to be a Christian community, but it leads us to explore the ways in which people come to faith.

The language of 'gathered church' can be very sharply articulated and the church is perceived as a community circumscribed by a clear boundary. On this border between the two spheres of church and world there are clear dues to be paid even when a person is carrying the passport of faith. Yet recent missiological investigation and reflection highlight the way in which many adult converts in Britain come to faith as the culmination of a journey which lasts years and which involves their participation in worship and church life before the threshold of personal faith commitment is crossed.[18]

A recent attempt to respond to this missiological reality within the Baptist tradition is the suggestion of Keith Jones that the notion 'gathered church' be replaced by the term 'gathering church'.[19] This does not in itself resolve the tensions of identity and relevance but it does move the debate forward by claiming that the very church identity which needs to be safeguarded is one which should be missionary by intent. While it continues to distinguish sharply this kind of church from Christendom models, and it is significant that Jones' suggestion is made in the context of a discussion of the continental Anabaptists, it portrays the gathered community as an including community rather than an excluding one.[20] The confessional *centre* of the church is identified more clearly than its circumference is delineated.

Jones' presentation of the Anabaptists also raises the challenge of discipleship and this in turn can provide a theological under-girding for the shift from 'gathered' to 'gathering'. Once discipleship becomes a leading model of what it means to be a Christian believer, a shift in focus takes place from the purity of the church to the life of believers in the world. Doing God's will is not only about preserving the church as a spotless bride of Christ but of being obedient in the activities and relationships of, for example, work and family. Such concerns were integral to some parts of the Reformation and the so-called 'Protestant work ethic' is a good example of this shift in focus beyond the church. It has been argued that much of the Reformation was a lay movement[21] and the emphasis on daily living reflects this just as clearly as debates about ministry and lay leadership in the governance of the church.

However, models of church still inform the way in which churches of the Reformation have interpreted this engagement with the whole of life. After all, the medieval church engaged with the whole of life, though the Reformers criticized the way in which that engagement was enacted. Yet it can be argued that many of the continental reformers adopted a similar Christendom model of the relationship of church and society for they also sought to control behaviour in civic society, though now it was based on what they perceived to be biblical principles. The vision of a gathered church challenged these assumptions of the church prescribing and proscribing behaviour for citizens.

The vision of a gathering, rather than gathered, church continues to place responsibility *within* the Christian community, but the way in which its members live in the world subtly shifts from exile to pilgrimage—a pilgrimage which they encourage others to share. Church life then is not seen as the sphere of perfection but as the sphere of formation—a place where we engage not in personal fulfilment or ecclesial being but in the process of becoming. Such a vision would fit well with Bonhoeffer's category of the 'penultimate'.[22] This eschatological approach to ecclesiology offers fertile ground for a missiological spirituality both for individuals in their daily living and for the Christian community. Within the church, the gathering of believers is thus recognized as the work of God, for 'gathering' is theologically a verb before it is a noun. God gathers the *ekklesia* and that very community is dependent upon divine grace and the activity of the Spirit both in the gathering together and the ministries of the community once gathered. Both missiology and ecclesiology may be seen as aspects of eschatology because they are the fruit of pneumatology!

Further, the notion of a 'gathering' church carries within it a dynamic which resists solidifying into a static institution. The movement of gathering is balanced by a dispersing of the community into the world. For many Baptists, the great commission of Matthew 28 has had such symbolic importance and this is liturgically expressed whenever at the end of a worship service the dismissal and blessing are seen as a communal commissioning. Attention to Christ means we cannot 'stay and sing' but must return to the fray as faithful witnesses. Mission is not only, and not even primarily, to be found in organized ecclesial mission projects, but in the interface of church and world as each believer lives their priestly calling in the world.

A significant missiological and pastoral challenge for all churches is to develop a missional vision which does not limit the horizon of the *missio dei* to the gathered church and places sufficient importance on the dispersed mode of ecclesial being and activity. There is rightly an emphasis on drawing new converts into the Christian community for worship, fellowship, pastoral care and formation. However, there has not been sufficient attention paid to the life of Christian believers at work, at home or in the public arena. A missional understanding of dispersal, coupled to a notion of a gathering, rather than gathered, church might offer ways of addressing this imbalance.

Since the Lausanne Conference of 1975 evangelicals, including Baptists, have given greater attention to what is often called 'holistic' mission. This has take various forms but at its heart is a recognition that acts of compassion, or prophetic statements concerning justice are not means towards an evangelistic end, but are examples of God's mission. Thus the relationship of evangelism to mission is configured in a way that sees 'mission' as the outworking of God's kingdom purposes and 'evangelism' as one aspect, albeit a very important aspect, of that larger mission.[23]

A British Baptist expression of this missional configuration is the document *5 Core Values for a Gospel People* which both expressed a movement in the 1990s and continues to influence churches in the subsequent decade. Here the quality of church life is addressed and cluster of values affirmed: churches are to be missionary, prophetic, inclusive, sacrificial and worshipping communities—not in order to achieve something else, but because these values are an embodiment of the gospel in communal form. Being the gospel is given precedence over speaking the gospel, though it is acknowledged that being will lead to doing. Here mission flows from what the church is—a community shaped by the gospel of Jesus Christ.

4. A spirituality of grace and the mission of God

There are a number of contemporary issues which lead us to question the healthiness of mission in many Baptist churches. The list is not new but bears repeating if we are to reach any kind of diagnosis, let alone identify a remedy.

First, there is the activism which permeates large sections of church life. Much remains to be achieved and the burden of achieving is placed firmly on the shoulders of the Christian community. David Bebbington has identified activism as one of the four primary characteristics of evangelicalism[24] and Baptist church life is often very evangelical in this regard. Attention to Christ and a responsibility for service and witness are essential characteristics of faithful Christian living, but these need to be seen within an adequate theological framework where the life and mission of the triune God is given central place.

Second, there is the tendency to be pragmatic in the practice of designing and leading worship. Missional pragmatism entered evangelical worship in a significant way when Charles Finney, in the middle of the nineteenth century, adapted the practices of the Kentucky camp meetings towards a programmatic and evangelistic use of worship. This pragmatism remains a feature of evangelical worship whenever the worship experience is used as a means of encouraging a faith commitment on the part of the worshippers. Liturgically and pastorally, such pragmatism can be defended if the central feature of the worship event is the worshipping of God as revealed in Christ and the scriptures. However, if the tail wags the dog and worship is used *instrumentally* in order to facilitate conversions, rather than to glorify God, then a misplaced missionary zeal has undermined the greatest service of the Christian church, the worship of God.

Third, a concern for numerical success can lead churches to pin their hopes on evangelistic programmes before an exploration of discipleship. Here lie twin dangers. On the one hand, there is the dependence on formulaic and programmatic packages which have achieved 'success' elsewhere over and against the faith-living experimentation of what God might be calling this particular community to do in this particular situation, its unique mission context. On the other hand, there can be an exalting of conversion over the call to faithful discipleship. Arguably, however gradual the process of coming to faith might be for any person, there will nonetheless be a crossing of a threshold from seeking to finding, or being found. Yet conversion is more than a cognitive or even affective shift from doubt or uncertainty to faith. Conversion is also the conversion of a life lived in honour of self to a life lived to the glory of God. The liminal nature of conversion is important but it is an over-simplification if that liminality is narrowed to a transactional understanding of being a Christian. Being 'in' or 'out' of the household of faith may be an important metaphor, but so is the growth in grace or rootedness in Christ.

To these general dangers we need to add one which is specific to church leaders and ministers, namely, the vocational uncertainty they experience in a changing world. The decline of institutional religion in the West has accentuated this feature of ministerial life. An historical survey of the literature of pastoral theology in the twentieth century would highlight a continuing search for identity as the role of the pastoral leader has changed in response to sociological trends. Sometimes there has been little theological attempt to undergird pragmatic changes in the role of ministers, whether the leading image is counsellor, manager or leader. To this general context there is always to be added the pressures on individual ministers as they seek to justify their vocational existence in a world which requires outcomes to be measurable.[25] Activism, pragmatism and the need for personal affirmation and evident fruit are heavy taskmasters and dangerous guides. For the minister, the burden is heavy and the risk of burnout not inconsiderable. For the church, there is the danger of doing 'the right deed for the wrong reason',[26] as T.S. Eliot's Becket puts it succinctly, of engaging in mission out of insecurity or institutional fear rather than as a participation in the redeeming and gracious flow of the love of God.

The story of Baptist life has frequently involved a conversation with and within Calvinism. I am not arguing for a return to a rigid Calvinistic past, or even the theological systems which characterized much of eighteenth and nineteenth century debates. However, I am suggesting that there are a number of spiritual challenges in relation to worship and mission which would be positively addressed if we re-affirmed and entered into a stronger and deeper sense of the grace of God.

Here we are back to the conjunction of theology, prayer and practical Christian living. The practice of mission drives us to our knees in prayer for divine assistance. But it should also flow out of a love for the world, which itself flows from a communion with God which transforms our affections and values. Further, it is only when we grasp the place of mission within the overflowing love of Father, Son and Holy Spirit that we can see rightly the role, rather than the task, to which we are called: namely, partners in redemption and participators in the divine love, which leads to the divine going to the far country. As we consider motivations for mission, a powerful impulse must be passionate love, caught from God and directed to others. What Eduard Thurneysen says of pastoral care is also true of missionary activity: it 'has as its only content the communication of the forgiveness of sins in Jesus Christ'.[27] The mission of the church is to announce the kingdom of God and initiate women and men into that kingdom.[28]

We might argue that the doctrinal centre of this truth is the doctrine of the Trinity, with its vision of God in communion, of the divine love overflowing into redemption for the world. Yet the doctrinal expression of the *human experience* of this truth must be the undeserved grace of God. Here is the key to unlock the shackles of activism and insecurity. Here is the word of command to free ministers from drivenness and churches from misguided faddism. The fundamental motivation for mission is the experience of sheer grace, and the desire to share grace with others. Christians have always struggled with the issue of assurance; yet grace remains amazing, simple words of forgiveness and promise can still offer hope. More particularly, the grace of God is both the *message* of the evangelist and the *liberation* of the mission worker. I am convinced that the primary spiritual challenge for ministers and other church workers is to accept and appropriate the word of grace which they so readily offer to others.

This is far more than a ministerial survival strategy: it is true theology and authentic Christian devotion. It is only from the vantage point of grace that we can see God as God truly is and it is only from this starting point that we can engage in *Christian* mission, the mission of God. For what the church offers in evangelism is not only its message but its very self. The community of disciples and the evangelists who represent it must be shaped by the gospel—that is, shaped by grace—if the true gospel is to be preached.

5. Liturgical spirituality

I return again to Sheldrake's notion of conjunction. There is an interrelatedness necessary for healthy spirituality, a mutual feeding of prayer, thought and action. Each of these three spheres needs the other two if there is to be health. This applies not only to individual Christian living but to the communal reality of life in the body of Christ. But in both personal and communal expressions of spirituality we may ask which is the best way to enter the circle and transform its parts. There is, of course no one answer, but because we are addressing the question of healthy mission, it will be helpful to address the other two spheres—thought, or doctrine, and prayer—in order to see how the interrelatedness makes a difference to mission.

Thus the two themes of holy living and grace which have been highlighted may be seen as doctrinal ones in which a focus on right thought (*orthodoxy*) might lead to right action (*orthopraxy*). The concept of the ecclesial heart of mission as a gathering community enables us to recognize the pneumatological nature of mission, understanding it to be the mission of God; this leads to a practical relating of life in the church to the whole of life, as a holistic holiness. Similarly, a doctrinal emphasis on grace will both offer hope to burden-carrying witnesses, and lead to a more holistic witness in which the word of grace uttered is embodied in a grace-filled and grace-freed community.

But, to stretch the body metaphor in a biologically bizarre way—head reaches hands through the heart! Doctrine is for most Christians appropriated through prayer and worship. It is in our regular relating to God and in the formational singing and celebrating of the faith that what we believe influences both what we feel and what we do. So the challenge for worship leaders and ministers is to enable these dimensions of gathering and grace to find constant expression in the worship of the community.

For gathering, this will mean a focus on the activity of God in the lives of the worshippers—the God who gathers through the dynamic influence of the Holy Spirit, the God who gathers a community for mutual support and affirmation, the God who gathers is at work even in non-ecclesiastical environments. There will be focus on the whole of life for the God who gathers is the one who disperses and blesses. The God who gathers, does so through the scattering of the community into individual and sometimes lonely witnesses whose life in the Spirit is a part of the gathering of God. Such a vision needs to be shared in worship, just as that worship needs to offer support for those lonely witnesses through prayer, testimony and exhortation. The vision of God which such themes express is a vision of omnipresence and faithfulness, of outpouring love and dynamic action. So eschatology leads to faith and hope and, therefore, to healthy mission.

For grace, this will mean a constant focus on the gospel of Jesus Christ and the outflowing love of the triune God. Prayers of confession and words of assurance of forgiveness are a pastorally necessary starting point, yet often they are missing in Baptist worship. Life in the Spirit is life lived in and through grace and an increased awareness of what God does in worship will be an antidote to an activism which finds its liturgical expression in a striving which can lead to manipulation and exhaustion. Contemporary Baptists would do well to reflect on the phrase 'a means of grace' and ask themselves where in worship God offers places for God's own presence to be encountered in life-changing ways. More particularly, baptism and the Lord's Supper, preaching and prayer need to be events in which we expect God to be the primary agent.

For mission to be influenced by worship, the conjunction with a true vision of God is vital. The vision of a gathering God should avoid the temptation to luxuriate in warm experiences—and the personal and repeated appropriation of divine grace should warm hearts to the mission imperative that springs from love rather than duty, from faith and hope in a faithful God rather than the latest formula or human striving. Spirituality is 'life in the Spirit'[29] and both worship and mission are only truly Christian when this reality is celebrated.

Notes

[1] H. Wheeler Robinson, *The Life and Faith of the Baptists*. Revised Edition (London: Kingsgate Press, 1947), p. 118.

[2] http://www.bwanet.org/AboutUs/Vision.htm, accessed 30.4.06.

[3] Philip Sheldrake, *Spirituality and History: Questions of Interpretation and Method* (London: SPCK, 1995), p. 60.

[4] C. Booth, *Life and Labour of the People of London* (London: Macmillan, 1903), Vol. 7, p. 125.

[5] See Roger Hayden, *English Baptist History and Heritage*. Revised Edition (Didcot: Baptist Union of Great Britain, 2005), p. 27.

[6] Deep-seated convictions are evident in the exchange of pamphlets about hymn singing which occurred between 1785 and 1787 between Gilbert Boyce of the old General Baptists and Dan Taylor, whom he had previously baptized.

[7] See Christopher J. Ellis, *Gathering: A Theology and Spirituality of Worship in Free Church Tradition* (London: SCM Press, 2004), p. 96.

[8] See Ian M. Randall, *The English Baptists of the Twentieth Century* (Didcot: Baptist Historical Society, 2005) pp. 34-36.

[9] I. Stackhouse, *The Gospel-Driven Church: Retrieving Classical Ministries for Contemporary Revivalism* (Carlisle: Paternoster, 2004).

[10] *5 Core Values for a Gospel People* (Didcot: Baptist Union of Great Britain, no date).

[11] See Ellis, *Gathering*, pp. 203-6.

[12] For the Separatists and early Baptists a divine ordinance was to be found in scripture. However, it not only included explicit commands but also what were perceived to be precedents and examples which were to be followed by the Christian community. See Ellis, *Gathering*, p. 76f.

[13] Jürgen Moltmann, *The Crucified God* (London: SCM Press, 1974), pp. 7-28, especially p. 25.

[14] A. C. Underwood, *A History of the English Baptists* (London: Carey Kingsgate Press, 1947), pp. 15ff.

[15] W. L. Lumpkin, *Baptist Confessions of Faith* (Valley Forge: Judson Press, 1969), p. 166.

[16] B. R. White, *Association Records of the Particular Baptists of England, Wales and Ireland to 1660*, (London: Baptist Historical Society, 1971). p. 56.

[17] For church as messianic community, see Jürgen Moltmann, *The Church in the Power of the Spirit: A Contribution to Messianic Ecclesiology* (London: SCM Press, 1977), p. 196.

[18] See John Finney, *Finding Faith Today: How does it happen?* (Swindon: British and Foreign Bible Society, 1992) and Grace Davie, *Religion in Britain since 1945: Believing without Belonging* (Oxford: Blackwell, 1994).

[19] Keith G. Jones, *A Believing Church: Learning from some Contemporary Anabaptist and Baptist Perspectives* (Didcot: Baptist Union of Great Britain, 1998), p. 38f. and p. 64.

[20] This is certainly resonant of contemporary Baptist concerns as the church as an inclusive community is another of the core values articulated in the 1990s. See *5 Core Values*.

[21] See Alister E. McGrath, *The Intellectual Origins of the European Reformation* (Oxford: Basil Blackwell, 1987), pp. 10-12, and *Roots that Refresh: A Celebration of Reformation Spirituality* (London: Hodder and Stoughton, 1991), p. 44f.

[22] Dietrich Bonhoeffer, *Ethics* (London: SCM Press, 1955), pp. 103ff.

[23] For an eschatological interpretation of evangelism, see William Abraham, *The Logic of Evangelism* (Grand Rapids: Eerdmans, 1989).

[24] David W. Bebbington, *Evangelicalism in Modern Britain: A History from the 1730s to the 1980s* (London: Unwin Hyman, 1989), pp. 10-12.

[25] See further, 'The Discovery of Pastoral Identity' in T. C. Oden, *Pastoral Theology: Essentials of Ministry* (New York: HarperCollins, 1983), pp. 3-17;

Theological Foundations for Ministry, (Edinburgh: T. & T. Clark, 1979), and I. Stackhouse, *Gospel-Driven Church,* especially pp. 220-253.

[26] *Collected Poems and Plays of T. S. Eliot* (London: Faber and Faber, 1969), p. 258.

[27] Quoted in A. Purves, *Reconstructing Pastoral Theology: A Christological Foundation* (Louisville and London: Westminster/John Knox, 2004), p. 175.

[28] For evangelism as initiation into the kingdom of God, see Abraham, *The Logic of Evangelism*.

[29] Sheldrake, *Spirituality and History*, p. 45, and Gordon D. Fee, *Listening to the Spirit in the Text* (Grand Rapids: Eerdmans/ Vancouver, British Columbia: Regent College Publishing, 2000), pp. 3-15.

Index